AF371507

Freeze Drying Cookbook for Preppers

Tasty Recipes for Survival on a Budget with **Simple Directions**

Noah Wood

Introduction

There are various methods of food preservation. One of them is freeze drying. This method removes water from a particular food item while at the same time preserving its taste and nutrients. Freeze-dried food items are lightweight and can be stored for over twenty-five years. It is a kind of dehydration technique that is very different from freezing. There are two steps in the freeze-drying process. The first step includes freezing the food below its glass transition temperature. Then a vacuum is applied, removing all the food's moisture. The moisture is already converted to ice in the freezing stage, so applying vacuum is directly converted to vapors. This method has an advantage over other preservation methods as it does not require high temperature; therefore, you don't have to worry about the degradation of heat-sensitive components in the food. Freeze drying can be done either using a freeze-dryer machine or without a machine. However, freeze-drying your food without a freeze-dryer is usually complicated. Also, a freeze dryer machine is probably the best option if you have to freeze dry your food on a large scale. It comes with different freeze dryer trays suitable for different kinds of food. However, it would be best if you remembered that freeze drying is a time taking process. Depending upon the type of food, it may also take several hours to days. Therefore, if you need to store your food quickly, you should probably go for some other method of food preservation, such as pressure canning, water bath canning, etc.

Table of Content:

Chapter 1: Meat Recipes

1. Freeze Dried Chicken Pot Pie

Ready in: 55 minutes

Servings: 24

Difficulty: Medium

INGREDIENTS

For the Crust

- 2 ½ cups flour

- 1 tsp. sugar

- 1 cup water

- 1 cup cold butter

- 1 tsp. salt

For the Filling

- 1 tsp. salt

- 1 cup flour

- 2 cups evaporated milk

- 2 cups onions

- 2 cups celery

- 2/3 cup butter

- 4 cups bone broth

- 2 cups peas

- 2 cups carrots

- 8 cups chicken

- 1 tsp. pepper

DIRECTIONS

1. Blend sugar, flour, salt and cold butter together in a blender.

2. Add cold water and blend till the mixture starts to set.

3. Remove the mixture from the blender and knead it gently to form a dough.

4. Make four dough balls and place them in the freezer for twenty minutes.

5. Remove the dough and roll it. Then, use the ring of the mason jar to cut circles.

6. Transfer the circular pieces of dough to the cookie sheet and bake for five minutes at 375 Fahrenheit.

7.   Prepare the filling by first melting butter in a pan. Add chicken, and once it's almost done, add the veggies.

8.   Add remaining butter and sprinkle the mixture with flour.

9.   Stir and add broth along with the cream.

10.   Stir for a few minutes and then add frozen peas, salt and pepper and stir for a few more minutes. Turn off the heat.

11.   Add the chicken pie filling to freeze-dryer trays.

12.   Place baked mini pie crusts onto the separate freeze-dryer tray.

13.   Allow the filling and crust to freeze dry completely.

14.   Transfer the filling to six mason jars and crumble a mini pie crust on top of each.

15.   Add an oxygen absorber to each jar and place the lids on top.

16.   To eat: Add 1 cup of boiled water to the jar and shake gently. Serve and enjoy!

NUTRITION: Calories: 274 kcal Fat: 17 g Protein: 9 g Carbs: 20g

2. Garlic Lime Chicken

Ready in: 30 minutes

Servings: 4

Difficulty: Easy

INGREDIENTS

- 3 tbsp. lime juice

- 1 tbsp. olive oil

- 4 boneless, skinless chicken breast halves

- ¼ tsp. dried thyme

- ¼ tsp. garlic powder

- ¼ tsp. cayenne pepper

- ¾ tsp. salt

- 2 tsp. garlic powder

- 2 tbsp. butter

- ¼ tsp. dried parsley

- 1/8 tsp. onion powder

- 1/8 tsp. paprika

- ¼ tsp. black pepper

DIRECTIONS

1. Add salt, black pepper, paprika, cayenne pepper, onion powder, parsley, garlic powder and thyme in a bowl and mix well.

2. Rub the spice mixture on both sides of the chicken breasts.

3. Take a pan and heat butter and olive oil in it.

4. Add chicken and sauté for five minutes per side.

5. Add lime juice and garlic powder and cook for five more minutes.

6. Turn off the heat and let it cool.

7. Cut the chicken into strips and place it in freeze dryer trays and allow it to freeze dry completely.

8. Transfer chicken to mason jars.

9. Add an oxygen absorber to each jar and close the lids.

10. NUTRITION: Calories: 220 kcal Fat: 10.7 g Protein: 27.7 g Carbs: 2.4g

3. Pork Cassoulet

Ready in: 2 hours 30 minutes

Servings: 4

Difficulty: Difficult

INGREDIENTS

- 400 g haricot or cannellini beans

- 2 rosemary stalks

- 600 ml stock

- 1 tsp. fennel seeds

- 10 fat garlic cloves

- 350 g assorted diced pork

- ¾ cup finely chopped parsley

- 1 tbsp. tomato puree

- 2 tbsp. red wine vinegar

- 1 thinly sliced carrot

- 1 sliced onion

- 4 tbsp. fat

- Drizzle of oil

- Few tbsp. dried breadcrumbs

- 1 cup of green vegetables

DIRECTIONS

1. Allow the oven to preheat.

2. Heat an ovenproof pan and add fat and diced meat to it. Cook for a few minutes.

3. Add sliced onion, garlic cloves, carrot and fennel seeds to the pan and cook on low heat.

4. Add red wine vinegar, tomato puree, stock, parsley, and rosemary in it and bring to a boil.

5. Let the mixture simmer for ten minutes.

6. Place the pan in the oven for one and a half hours.

7. Add beans to it and bake for another thirty minutes.

8. Remove the pan and add veggies and breadcrumbs. Drizzle oil and let it cook in the oven for five more minutes.

9. Transfer the cassoulet to freeze dryer trays and place it in a freeze dryer.

10. Allow it to freeze dry completely.

11.   Transfer to an airtight container and add an oxygen absorber.

12.   Close the lid and store in a cool, dry place.

NUTRITION: Calories: 501 kcal Fat: 30 g Protein: 28 g Carbs: 26g

4. Freeze Dried Chicken Curry

Ready in: 50 minutes

Servings: 3

Difficulty: Medium

INGREDIENTS

- 2 tbsp. coriander leaves

- ½ cup hot water

- ½ tsp. salt

- ¼ cup yogurt

- ½ cup tomatoes

- 1 tbsp. ginger garlic paste

- 2 green chilies

- 1cup chopped onions

- 2 tbsp. oil

- ½ kg chicken

- Spice powders

- 1 tsp. coriander

- 1 tsp. garam masala

- 1 tsp. red chili powder

- ¼ tsp. turmeric powder

Whole spices

- 3 green cardamoms

- 2-inch cinnamon piece

- 4 cloves

- 1 bay leaf

DIRECTIONS

1. Heat oil in a pan and add whole spices. Fry them till there is an aroma.

2. Add onions and chilies and fry for a few minutes.

3. Add ginger garlic paste and fry for a few more seconds.

4. Add turmeric, salt and tomatoes to the pan and stir.

5. Add yogurt, red chili powder, garam masala and coriander powder and cook the mixture on low flame.

6. Add chicken and coriander leaves and fry for three minutes.

7. Cover the pan and let the chicken cook on low flame for a few minutes.

8.   Add ½ cup of boiled water to the pan and cook on medium flame.

9.   Turn off the heat and add coriander leaves for garnishing.

10.   Transfer the chicken curry to freeze dryer trays and place in a freeze dryer.

11.   Allow it to freeze dry completely.

12.   Transfer the curry to airtight containers and add an oxygen absorber.

13.   Close the lids and store them in a cool, dry place.

NUTRITION: Calories: 417 kcal Fat: 26 g Protein: 33 g Carbs: 10g

5. Tuscan Chicken Pasta Bake

Ready in: 45 minutes

Servings: 6

Difficulty: Medium

INGREDIENTS

- 1 cup shredded mozzarella cheese

- 1 cup milk

- 7 oz. julienne cut sun-dried tomatoes packed in oil

- minced garlic clove

- 1.25 lbs. boneless skinless chicken breasts, cut into bite-sized pieces

- ½ cup grated Parmesan cheese

- 3 oz. reduced-fat cream cheese

- 5 oz. fresh baby kale

- 1 diced onion

- 13.25 oz. whole wheat penne pasta

DIRECTIONS

1. Preheat the oven to 350 Fahrenheit.

2. Take a large baking dish and spray it with cooking spray.

3. Cook pasta as directed on the package.

4. Add 1 tbsp. of reserved sundried tomato oil in a pan and add chicken and onions

5. Cook chicken and onions for five minutes and add garlic. Cook for one more minute.

6. Add kale and sundried tomatoes and cook for a few more minutes.

7. Add cream cheese, milk, and parmesan cheese and stir.

8. Add pasta and mix well.

9. Transfer the pasta to a baking dish and add mozzarella cheese on top.

10. Bake the pasta for thirty minutes.

11. Remove the pasta and let cool.

12. Transfer it to freeze-drying trays and place it in a freeze-dryer.

13. Allow the pasta to freeze dry completely.

14. Transfer to airtight containers and add an oxygen absorber.

15. Close the lids and store them in a cool, dry place.

NUTRITION: Calories: 361 kcal Fat: 13 g Protein: 41 g Carbs: 19g

6. Slow Cooker Pepper Steak

Ready in: 3 hours 30 minutes

Servings: 6

Difficulty: Difficult

INGREDIENTS

- 1 tsp. salt

- 1 tsp. white sugar

- 3 tbsp. soy sauce

- 14.5 oz. stewed tomatoes

- 2 chopped green bell peppers

- ½ cup chopped onion

- 1 tbsp. cornstarch

- ¼ cup hot water

- 1 cube beef bouillon

- 3 tbsp. vegetable oil

- ¾ tbsp. garlic powder

- 2 lb. beef sirloin, cut into strips

DIRECTIONS

1. Sprinkle the beef strips with garlic powder. 2 Take a pan and heat the oil in it. Add beef strips and cook for five minutes per side.

3. Transfer the beef strips to a slow cooker.

4. Add hot water and cornstarch to a separate bowl and mix well.

5. Pour the cornstarch mixture into the slow cooker and add onions, stewed tomatoes, bell peppers, sugar, salt and soy sauce. Mix well.

6. Let the mixture simmer for three hours on high flame.

7. Transfer the mixture to freeze dryer trays lined with parchment paper and place in a freeze dryer.

8. Allow it to freeze dry completely.

9. Transfer the freeze-dried pepper steak to airtight containers and add an oxygen absorber.

10. Close the lid and store in a cool, dry place.

NUTRITION: Calories: 301 kcal Fat: 15.8 g Protein: 28.2 g Carbs: 11.7 g

7. Fish Sticks

Ready in: 25 minutes

Servings: 2

Difficulty: Easy

INGREDIENTS

- Butter-flavoured cooking spray

- 1 large egg, beaten

- ½ tsp. lemon-pepper seasoning

- ½ tsp. salt

- ¾ lb. cod fillets

- ½ cup all-purpose flour

- ½ tsp. paprika

- ½ cup dried breadcrumbs

DIRECTIONS

1.   Allow the oven to preheat to 400 Fahrenheit.

2.   Add breadcrumbs and seasoning to a bowl and mix.

3.   Add eggs and flour to separate bowls and set aside.

4.   Take fish fillets and dip them in flour first, then in egg and then in crumb mixture.

5.   Take a baking sheet and coat it with cooking spray.

6   Place the fillets on the baking sheet and bake for ten minutes.

7.   Remove the fillets and let them cool.

8.   Transfer them to freeze dryer trays and place them in a freeze dryer.

9.   Allow them to freeze dry completely.

10.   Transfer them to airtight containers and add an oxygen absorber.

11.   Close the lids and store them in a cool, dry place.

NUTRITION: Calories: 278 kcal Fat: 4 g Protein: 33 g Carbs: 25 g

8. Chicken Cacciatore

Ready in: 50 minutes

Servings: 6

Difficulty: Medium

INGREDIENTS

- ½ tsp. red pepper flakes

- 2 tbsp. tomato paste

- 150 ml red wine

- 2 tbsp. freshly chopped parsley and basil

- ½ cup pitted black olives

- 1 large, sliced carrot

- 1 small, diced yellow bell pepper

- 1 diced medium onion

- 6 bone-in skinless chicken thighs

- 7 oz. halved Roma tomatoes

- 28 oz. crushed tomatoes

- 1 tsp. dried oregano

- 8 sprigs thyme

- 10 oz. sliced mushrooms

- 2 diced red bell pepper

- 2 tbsp. minced garlic

- ¾ tsp. salt

- ¾ tsp. pepper

- 3 tbsp. olive oil

DIRECTIONS

1. Sprinkle salt and pepper over the chicken.

2. Take a pan and heat the oil in it. Add chicken and cook for four minutes per side.

3. Add remaining oil to the pan, onion, and garlic and cook for a few more minutes.

4. Add peppers, mushrooms, herbs, and carrots and cool for five minutes.

5. Add wine and cook for two minutes on low heat.

6. Add crushed tomatoes, Roma tomatoes, chili flakes, salt, pepper, and tomato paste. Cover the pan and cook for forty minutes on low flame.

7. Add olives and cook for ten more minutes.

8. Add parsley and basil for garnishing.

9.   Transfer the chicken cacciatore to freeze-drying trays and place in a freeze dryer.

10.   Allow it to freeze dry completely.

11.   Transfer the cacciatore to an airtight container and add an oxygen absorber.

12.   Close the lid and store in a cool, dry place.

NUTRITION: Calories: 310 kcal Fat: 11 g Protein: 27 g Carbs: 22g

9. Shrimp Stir Fry

Ready in: 30 minutes

Servings: 4

Difficulty: Easy

INGREDIENTS

Stir Fry Sauce

- 1 tbsp. cornstarch

- 1 tsp. sriracha

- 1 tbsp. honey

- 2 tbsp. soy sauce

- 1 tsp. sesame oil

- 2 tsp. rice vinegar

- 2 tbsp. Shaoxing wine

- ½ cup low-sodium chicken broth

Stir Fry

- 1 tsp. sesame seeds

- 1 tbsp. minced garlic

- 1 ½ cup chopped bell pepper

- 1 ½ cups small broccoli florets

- 1 pinch salt

- 2 tsp. minced ginger

- ½ cup chopped green onions

- 5 oz. snow peas

- 3 tbsp. vegetable oil

- 1 lb. large shrimp

DIRECTIONS

1. Add chicken broth, Shaoxing wine, rice vinegar, sesame oil, cornstarch, sriracha, honey and soy sauce in a small bowl and mix well to prepare the sauce.

2. Heat oil in a pan and add shrimp and salt to it. Cook for two minutes per side.

3. Transfer the shrimp to the plate and add the remaining oil to the pan.

4. Add broccoli and fry.

5. Add snow peas, bell pepper and green onions and cook for three to four minutes.

6. Add garlic and ginger to it and sauté for a few seconds.

7. Pour the sauce over the veggies in the pan and mix.

8.   Add shrimp to the pan and stir.

9.   Sprinkle with sesame seeds and turn off the heat.

10.   Transfer the shrimp stir fry to freeze dryer trays and place in a freeze dryer.

11.   Allow it to freeze dry completely.

12.   Transfer the freeze-dried shrimp stir fry to airtight containers and add an oxygen absorber.

13.   Close the lids and store them in a cool, dry place.

NUTRITION: Calories: 292 kcal Fat: 13 g Protein: 20 g Carbs: 21g

10. Sweet and Sour Pork

Ready in: 2 hours

Servings: 4

Difficulty: Difficult

INGREDIENTS

- 1 lb. pork butt, cut into cubes

For Marinade

- 2 chopped green onions

- 1 egg white

- ¼ tsp. white sugar

- 1 tsp. salt

- 1 tsp. soy sauce

- For Frying

- ½ cup cornstarch

- 1-quart vegetable oil

Stir-Fried Vegetables

- 1 tbsp. cornstarch

- 8 oz. pineapple chunks

- ¼ tsp. salt

- ½ tsp. soy sauce

- ¼ cup ketchup

- 1/3 cup apple cider vinegar

- ¾ cup white sugar

- 1 ¼ cup of water

- 1 pinch salt

- 1 pinch of white sugar

- 1 medium onion

- 1 medium bell pepper

- 3 stalks celery

- 1 tbsp. vegetable oil

DIRECTIONS

1. Add pork, soy sauce, salt, green onions, egg whites, and sugar in a bowl and mix well. Cover the bowl and set aside for an hour.

2. Take a pan and heat the oil in it.

3. Take marinated pork cubes, coat them with cornstarch, and fry them in oil for ten minutes.

4. Heat oil in a wok and add vegetables. Cook for five minutes.

5. Add water, apple cider vinegar, sugar, soy sauce, ketchup and salt to a saucepan and bring to a boil.

6. Add pork cubes, pineapple chunks (with juice), and sauteed veggies.

7. Again, bring the mixture to a boil and add the remaining water and cornstarch.

8. Cook till the mixture thickens. Then turn off the heat.

9. Transfer it to freeze dryer trays and place it in a freeze dryer.

10. Allow it to freeze dry completely.

11. Transfer the freeze-dried sweet and sour pork to airtight containers and add an oxygen absorber.

12. Close the lids and store them in a cool, dry place.

NUTRITION: Calories: 663 kcal Fat: 35 g Protein: 13.9 g Carbs: 74.7 g

11. Sweet and Spicy Asian Meatballs

Ready in: 40 minutes

Servings: 4 ½ dozen

Difficulty: Medium

INGREDIENTS

- 2 lb. ground pork

- 2/3 cup panko breadcrumbs

- 1 tbsp. minced fresh ginger root

- 4 minced garlic cloves

- 3 tbsp. soy sauce

- 1 jalapeno pepper

- 3 tbsp. minced cilantro

- 1/3 cup sliced water chestnuts

- ½ medium onion

- 1 large egg

Sauce

- ½ cup thinly sliced green onions and toasted sesame seeds

- ½ tsp. Chinese five-spice powder

- 1 tbsp. toasted sesame oil

- 1 tbsp. Emeril's® Cajun Seasoning Blend

- 1 tbsp. minced fresh ginger root

- 3 minced garlic cloves

- 2 tbsp. Vietnamese chili garlic sauce

- 2 tbsp. fresh lime juice

- 3 tbsp. brown sugar

- 3 tbsp. honey

- ¼ cup Shaoxing rice wine

- 1/3 cup soy sauce

- ½ cup hoisin sauce

DIRECTIONS

1. Add egg, onion, water chestnuts, cilantro, jalapeno pepper, soy sauce, garlic cloves, gingerroot, breadcrumbs and pork in a bowl and mix well.

2.   Arrange the mixture into meatballs.

3.   Place the meatballs on greased wire racks.

4.   Place them in an air fryer and close the lid.

5.   Cook them in an air fryer for ten minutes. Try to cook in batches.

6.   In the meantime, prepare the sauce by adding all the ingredients to a bowl and mixing well.

7.   Place the meatballs in the inner pot and pour the sauce over them.

8   Again, cook them for two more minutes.

9.   Transfer the meatballs to freeze dryer trays and place them in a freeze dryer.

10.   Allow them to freeze dry completely.

11.   Transfer them to mason jars and add an oxygen absorber.

12.   Close the lids and store them in a cool, dry place.
        NUTRITION: Calories: 62 kcal Fat: 3 g Protein: 4 g Carbs: 4 g

12. Crab Cakes

Ready in: 25 minutes

Servings: 4

Difficulty: Easy

INGREDIENTS

- 1 tbsp. butter

- ½ cup crushed buttery round crackers

- 8 oz. crabmeat

- 1/8 tsp. red pepper flakes

- 1 tsp. dried tarragon

- 4 tsp. lemon juice

- 1 tbsp. minced green onions

- 3 tbsp. mayonnaise

- 1 egg

DIRECTIONS

1. Add mayonnaise, egg, green onions, tarragon, lemon juice and pepper flakes to a bowl and mix well.

2. Add crabmeat and stir.

3. Add cracker crumbs and mix again.

4. Make four patties from the mixture.

5 Take a pan and heat butter in it.

6. Fry the patties for about five minutes per side.

7. Transfer the patties to a freeze dryer tray and place them in a freeze dryer.

8. Allow them to freeze dry completely.

9. Transfer them to an airtight container and add an oxygen absorber.

10. Close the lid and store in a cool, dry place.

NUTRITION: Calories: 216 kcal Fat: 15.2 g Protein: 13.9 g Carbs: 5.7 g

13. Skillet Garlic Chicken Pasta

Ready in: 30 minutes

Servings: 4

Difficulty: Easy

INGREDIENTS

- ½ cup freshly grated parmesan cheese

- ½ tsp. lemon juice

- ½ tbsp. flour

- 2 tbsp. butter

- 1 pinch salt

- 1 pinch pepper

- 2 chicken breasts

- 1 cup heavy whipping cream

- ½ cup chicken broth

- 3 cloves garlic

- 1 tbsp. olive oil

- ½ tsp. garlic powder

- 8 oz. uncooked pasta

DIRECTIONS

1   Cook the pasta as directed on the package.

2.   Take chicken breasts and cut them in halves. Season them with salt, pepper and garlic powder.

3.   Take a pan and heat olive oil and butter in it.

4.   Add chicken breast halves and cook for five minutes.

5.   Remove the chicken pieces and set them aside.

6.   Add more butter to the pan and add flour and garlic to it. Stir for thirty minutes.

7.   Add chicken broth and lemon juice in it and bring to a boil.

8.   Add cream and cook for five more minutes.

9.   In the meantime, shred the chicken to pieces.

10.   Add chicken pieces, parmesan and cooked pasta to the pan and stir.

11.   Turn off the heat and let it cool.

12.   Transfer the pasta to freeze dryer trays and place in a freeze dryer.

13.   Allow it to freeze dry completely.

14.   Transfer the pasta to an airtight container and oxygen absorber.

15.   Close the lid and store in a cool, dry place.

NUTRITION: Calories: 689 kcal Fat: 39 g Protein: 38 g Carbs: 46g

14. Crock Pot Beef Fajitas

Ready in: 3 hours 15 minutes

Servings: 6

Difficulty: Difficult

INGREDIENTS

- ½ tsp. oregano

- 1 pinch salt

- 1 pinch pepper

- ½ tsp. ground coriander

- 1 tsp. paprika

- 1 tsp. granulated garlic

- 1 tsp. granulated onion

- 1 tsp. cumin

- 1 tbsp. chili powder

- 8 oz. diced tomatoes with chilies

- 6 cloves of garlic

- 2 large yellow onions

- 3 red bell peppers

- 2 tbsp. vegetable oil

- 1 ½ lb. flank steak

DIRECTIONS

1. Take steak and sprinkle it with salt and pepper.

2. Take a large pan and heat the oil in it.

3. Add steak to the pan and cook for three minutes per side.

4. Add onions, spices, salt, tomatoes, chilies, and garlic to a bowl and mix well.

5. Take a slow cooker pot and arrange half of the veggies at the bottom.

6. Place steak over the veggies and top with remaining veggies.

7. Cook for about three hours on high heat.

8. Turn off the heat, open the lid and let cool.

9. Transfer the beef fajitas to freeze dryer trays and place them in a freeze dryer.

10. Allow them to freeze dry completely.

11. Transfer the beef fajitas to an airtight container and add an oxygen absorber.

12. Close the lid and store in a cool, dry place.

NUTRITION: Calories: 598 kcal Fat: 22.8 g Protein: 28.2 g Carbs: 68.9 g

15. Mediterranean shrimp

Ready in: 10 minutes

Servings: 4

Difficulty: Easy

INGREDIENTS

- ¼ cup olive oil

- 1 slice of Feta cheese

- 3 tbsp. lemon juice

- 2 Lemon wedges

- 1 tsp. garlic

- Parsley as required

- 1/8 tsp. red pepper flakes

- 1 tsp. salt

- 1 lb. raw shrimp

- ¼ tsp. Black pepper

- ½ tsp. basil

- ½ tsp. oregano

DIRECTIONS

1. Take a bowl and mix in all the ingredients except shrimp.

2. By using the pepper towel, dry the shrimp.

3. Pour the prepared marinade over the shrimp and allow it to toss.

4. Place the marinated shrimp in the freezer.

5. Now allow the oven to preheat along with a lined baking sheet.

6. After removing from the freezer, allow the shrimp to broil for two minutes by flipping from all sides.

7. Once done, Remove shrimp from the broiler.

8. Serve at room temperature.

NUTRITION: Calories: 222 kcal Fat: 14.7 g Protein: 22.9 g Carbs: 1.3 g

16. Fettucine Alfredo with Chicken

Ready in: 5 minutes

Servings: 1

Difficulty: Easy

INGREDIENTS

- 1 pack of freeze-dried fettuccine alfredo with chicken

- ¼ cup water

DIRECTIONS

1. Open the mouth of the pouch and make it a bowl.

2. Add in boiling water and soak for 5 minutes.

3. Stir to settle all the contents in it and eat.

NUTRITION: Calories: 410 kcal Fat: 23 g Protein: 17 g Carbs: 32 g

17. Chicken Teriyaki with Rice

Ready in: 25 minutes

Servings: 4

Difficulty: Easy

INGREDIENTS

- 4 cup rice

- ½ cup sesame seeds and chopped green onions

- 3 tsp. cornstarch

- 2 tbsp. honey

- 2 tsp. minced garlic

- 1 tsp. ground ginger

- ½ tsp. sesame oil

- 2 tbsp. rice vinegar

- 3 tbsp. packed light brown sugar

- ½ cup water

- ½ cup low sodium soy sauce

- 1 tbsp. olive oil

- 4 boneless, skinless chicken breasts

DIRECTIONS

1. Take a large pan and heat the oil in it.

2. Add chicken cubes and cook till it turns brown.

3. In the meantime, prepare teriyakis sauce by adding water, soy sauce, brown sugar, honey, rice vinegar, sesame oil, cornstarch, ginger and garlic in a bowl and mix.

4. Pour the sauce over the chicken in the pan and cook till it thickens.

5. Turn off the heat and let it cool.

6. Transfer the teriyaki chicken to freeze dryer trays and add rice to a separate freeze dryer tray.

7. Place the trays in a freeze-dryer.

8. Allow them to freeze dry completely.

9. Transfer teriyaki chicken and rice to separate mason jars and add an oxygen absorber to each.

10. Close the lids and store them in a cool, dry place.

NUTRITION: Calories: 214 kcal Fat: 8.3 g Protein: 12 g Carbs: 23.9 g

18. Freeze Dried Bacon Bits

Ready in: 10 minutes

Servings: 8

Difficulty: Easy

INGREDIENTS

- 1 lb. bacon

- 1/8 tsp. black pepper

DIRECTIONS

1. Take bacon and cut it into small bits.

2. Season bacon bits with pepper.

3. Heat oil in a pan and add seasoned bacon bits.

4. Fry them for a few minutes.

5. Turn off the heat and let it cool.

6. Transfer the bacon bits to freeze dryer trays and place them in a freeze dryer.

7. Allow them to freeze dry completely.

8.   Transfer the freeze-dried bacon bits to mason jars and add an oxygen absorber.

9.   Close the lids and store them in a cool, dry place.

NUTRITION: Calories: 259.7 kcal Fat: 25.5 g Protein: 6.6 g Carbs: 0.4 g

19. Rosemary Shrimp

Ready in: 50 minutes

Servings: 4

Difficulty: Medium

INGREDIENTS

- ½ tsp. Cracked black pepper

- 3 cloves minced garlic

- 1/3 cup olive oil

- 1 lb. shrimp

- 1 tsp. kosher salt

- 2 tbsp. finely chopped rosemary

- 1 large lemon

DIRECTIONS

1. Add all the ingredients to a bowl and mix well.

2. Cover the bowl and set aside for thirty minutes.

3. Thread the shrimp onto skewers and grill them for three minutes per side.

4. Transfer the shrimps to freeze dryer trays and place them in a freeze dryer.

5. Allow them to freeze dry completely.

6. Transfer them to mason jars and add an oxygen absorber.

7. Close the lids and store them in a cool, dry place.

NUTRITION: Calories: 286 kcal Fat: 20 g Protein: 24 g Carbs: 4g

20. Chicken Alfredo with Pine Nuts

Ready in: 30 minutes

Servings: 8

Difficulty: Easy

INGREDIENTS

- 1 pinch salt

- ¼ cup freshly snipped Italian parsley

- 1 pinch pepper

- ¼ cup Alessi pine nuts

- 7 oz. Alessi julienne cut sun-dried tomatoes

- 8 oz. freshly shredded parmesan cheese

- 1 ½ cup heavy whipping cream

- 1 lb. ziti pasta

- 4 cups chicken stock

- 2 tsp. minced garlic

- 1 ½ lb. boneless, skinless chicken breasts

- 2 tbsp. salted butter

DIRECTIONS

1. Take a pan and heat butter in it. Add chicken pieces and cook them for a few minutes.

2. Remove the chicken from the pan and set it aside.

3. Add garlic to the pan and fry for a few seconds.

4. Pour chicken stock and bring it to a boil. Add pasta and cook for about eight minutes.

5. Add cream and chicken pieces and stir.

6. Let the mixture simmer for five minutes.

7. Add parmesan cheese to the pan while stirring continuously.

8. Add sun-dried tomatoes, salt and pepper and mix well.

9. Turn off the heat and add pine nuts, parsley and parmesan cheese.

10. Transfer the pasta to a freeze-dryer tray and place it in a freeze-dryer.

11. Allow it to freeze dry completely.

12. Transfer it to an airtight container and add an oxygen absorber.

13. Close the lid and store in a cool, dry place.

NUTRITION: Calories: 723 kcal Fat: 37 g Protein: 41 g Carbs: 55g

21. Chicken Fajita Bowl

Ready in: 30 minutes

Servings: 4

Difficulty: Easy

INGREDIENTS

- 2 large bell peppers

- 4 large chicken thighs, skinless and boneless

- 1 tbsp. fresh chopped cilantro

- 1 tsp. ground cumin

- 1 tsp. salt

- 1 tsp. ground chili

- 1 large, minced garlic clove

- 1 tbsp. oil

- 2 tbsp. freshly squeezed lime juice

Dressing

- 1 tsp. red chili flakes

- ½ tsp. salt

- ¼ tsp. ground cumin

- ½ tsp. brown sugar

- 1 tbsp. finely chopped cilantro

- 3 tbsp. freshly squeezed lime juice

- 2 tbsp. olive oil

DIRECTIONS

1. Add chicken, lime juice, cilantro, cumin, salt, oil, chili and garlic in a large bowl and mix well. Let stand for thirty minutes.

2. Take a large pan and heat the oil in it.

3. Place chicken in the pan and fry for eight minutes per side.

4. Transfer the chicken to the plate and add peppers to the pan.

5. Fry them for a few minutes. Add salt and pepper and stir.

6.   Slice chicken into strips and place it in the bowl.

7.   Add sauteed vegetables and mix.

8.   Prepare the dressing by mixing all the ingredients.

9.   Pour the dressing over the chicken and peppers in the bowl and mix well.

10.   Transfer the contents of the fajita bowl to freeze dryer trays and place them in a freeze dryer.

11.   Allow it to freeze dry completely.

12.   Transfer the freeze-dried chicken fajita to mason jars and add an oxygen absorber.

13.   Close the lid and store in a cool, dry place.

NUTRITION: Calories: 441 kcal Fat: 17 g Protein: 12 g Carbs: 47 g

22. Freeze Dried Shrimp

Ready in: 1 hour 10 minutes

Servings: 5

Difficulty: Difficult

INGREDIENTS

- 1 pinch of salt

- 1 pinch of Sichuan pepper

- 500 g fresh shrimp

- 1 minced garlic

- 1 tbsp. cooking wine

- 2 tbsp. vegetable oil

DIRECTIONS

1. Take a pan and heat the oil in it. Add Sichuan pepper and garlic and fry till fragrant.

2. Add shrimp and sprinkle with salt. Fry for ten minutes.

3. Add cooking wine and stir for two more seconds.

4. Turn off the heat and let it cool.

5. Transfer the shrimp to freeze dryer trays and place them in a freeze dryer.

6. Allow it to freeze dry completely.

7. Transfer the freeze-dried shrimp to a mason jar and add an oxygen absorber.

8. Close the lid and store in a cool, dry place.

NUTRITION: Calories: 220 kcal Fat: 20 g Protein: 24 g Carbs: 5g

23. Kathmandu Curry

Ready in: 25 minutes

Servings: 3

Difficulty: Easy

INGREDIENTS

- 1/8 bunch fresh coriander

- 2 cups water

- 4 tbsp. oil

- 5 garlic cloves

- ½ tsp. ginger

- 1 tbsp. garam masala

- ½ tsp. black pepper

- 1 tbsp. yogurt

- ¼ lemon juice

- 2 green chilies

- 1 tsp. salt

- 400g. crushed tomatoes

- 1tbsp.tahini

- 2 chicken breasts

DIRECTIONS

1. Take a large pan and heat the oil in it. Add onion and garlic to it and sauté for two minutes.

2. Add crushed tomatoes, chilies, tahini, salt, pepper, garam masala and yogurt and stir for a few seconds.

3. Add coriander and water and bring to a boil.

4. When the mixture starts to simmer, turn off the heat.

5. Heat oil in a separate pan and add sliced chicken breasts to it. Cook them for five minutes.

6. Transfer the chicken breasts to the sauce and stir.

7. Transfer the curry to freeze dryer trays and place in a freeze dryer.

8. Allow it to freeze dry completely.

9. Transfer it to airtight containers and add oxygen absorbers.

10. Close the lids and store them in a cool, dry place.

NUTRITION: Calories: 398 kcal Fat: 28 g Protein: 38 g Carbs: 14

24. Jamaican Style Jerk Chicken

Ready in: 3 hours 35 minutes

Servings: 8

Difficulty: Difficult

INGREDIENTS

Chicken Rub

- 1 tbsp. onion powder

- ½ tbsp. garlic powder

- 1 tbsp. Jerk seasoning

- 1 pinch salt

- 1 pinch pepper

- 1 whole chicken cut into pieces

Jerk Marinade

- 120 ml water or pineapple juice

- 1 tbsp. bouillon powder

- ½ tbsp. nutmeg

- 1 tbsp. cinnamon powder

- 2 tbsp. allspice

- 2 tbsp. brown sugar

- 1 ½ tbsp. soy sauce

- 4 chopped habanero pepper

- 1 ½ tbsp. chopped fresh ginger

- 6 roughly chopped garlic

- 3 chopped green onions

- 2 sprigs of fresh thyme

DIRECTIONS

1. Season chicken pieces with salt, pepper, jerk seasoning, onion powder and garlic powder and set aside.

2. Add thyme, green onions, garlic, ginger and habanero pepper in a blender and blend for thirty seconds.

3. Transfer these blended herbs to a bowl, add soy sauce, brown sugar, cinnamon, allspice, water or pineapple juice, nutmeg, and chicken bouillon, and mix well.

4. Add the seasoned chicken and set the chicken in the refrigerator to marinate.

5. Prepare the grill.

6. Remove the chicken from the refrigerator and place the pieces on the greased grill.

7.   Cook the chicken for twenty minutes while pouring the marinade over it from time to time.

8.   Transfer to a plate and let cool.

9.   Place the grilled chicken pieces on a freeze dryer tray and put them in a freeze dryer.

10.   Allow it to freeze dry completely.

11.   Transfer the freeze-dried chicken to mason jars and add oxygen absorbers.

12.   Close the lids and store them in a cool, dry place. NUTRITION: Calories: 84 kcal Fat: 1 g Protein: 2 g Carbs: 20 g

25. Backcountry Jambalaya

Ready in: 45 minutes

Servings: 6

Difficulty: Medium

INGREDIENTS

- ½ cup water

- 1 cube beef bouillon

- 1 cup pickled sausage slices

- 4 oz. packed chicken

- ½ tsp. paprika

- ¼ tsp. tomato bouillon

- ½ tsp. Cajun seasoning

- ½ tsp. cumin

- ½ tsp. freeze-dried garlic powder

- 1 tsp. dried onion flakes

- 2 tsp. dried bell pepper

- 1 tbsp. dried tomato flakes

- ¾ cup instant rice

- 1.5 oz. fuel

DIRECTIONS

11.   Take a large pan and heat the oil in it. Add sausage and cook for a few minutes.

12.   Add remaining ingredients and stir.

13.   Cover the pot and bring it to a boil.

14.   Cook the mixture till the rice is plump and the liquid is no more.

15.   Turn off the heat and let it cool.

16.   Transfer the jambalaya to freeze dryer trays and place it in a freeze dryer.

17.   Allow it to freeze dry completely.

18.   Transfer the freeze-dried jambalaya to an airtight container and add an oxygen absorber.

19.   Close the lid and store in a cool, dry place.

NUTRITION: Calories: 576 kcal Fat: 22 g Protein: 43 g Carbs: 46 g

26. Chicken Creole with Brown Rice

Ready in: 6 hours 15 minutes

Servings: 6

Difficulty: Difficult

INGREDIENTS

- ½ cup parsley

- 1 cup long grain brown rice

- ¼ cup tapioca starch

- 1 tbsp. Worcestershire sauce

- ¼ tsp. hot pepper sauce

- 1 tsp. paprika

- ½ tsp. thyme

- ¼ tsp. black pepper

- 3 whole cloves

- 2 tbsp. brown sugar

- 1 can of diced tomatoes

- 2 minced garlic cloves

- 1 cup diced carrot

- 1 cup diced celery

- 1 cup diced onion

- 1 cup diced green pepper

- 1 tbsp. canola oil

- 6 bone-in, skinless chicken breasts

DIRECTIONS

1. Take a large pan and heat the oil in it. Add chicken to the pan and cook until it turns brown.

2. Transfer the chicken to a slow cooker.

3. Add garlic, onions, green peppers, carrots and celery to the pan and fry them till they soften.

4. Add tomatoes, brown sugar, black pepper, tapioca, Worcestershire sauce, hot pepper sauce, paprika, thyme, and whole cloves in a bowl and mix.

5. Pour the sauce over the chicken in the slow cooker.

6. Cover the cooker and cook for six hours.

7. Cook rice according to the directions on the package.

8. Remove chicken from the slow cooker.

9. Add cooked rice to slow cooker and mix with sauce.

10. Transfer the rice to a dish and add chicken and sauteed vegetables.

11. Transfer the chicken creole and brown rice to a freeze-dryer tray and place in a freeze-dryer.

12. Allow them to freeze dry completely.

13. Transfer the freeze-dried creole with rice to an airtight container and add an oxygen absorber.

14. Close the lid and store in a cool, dry place.

NUTRITION: Calories: 440 kcal Fat: 7 g Protein: 50 g Carbs: 43g

27. Indian Vegetable Korma

Ready in: 40 minutes

Servings: 6

Difficulty: Easy

INGREDIENTS

- 1 lb. carrots

- 3 tbsp. olive oil

- ½ lb. potatoes

- 3 garlic cloves

- 1 head cauliflower

- 1-inch ginger

- 1 cup of green beans

- 1 onion

- 14 oz. tomatoes

- 1 cup cashews

- 2 tsp. salt

- 13.5 oz. coconut milk

- 1 tsp. cayenne powder

- 1 tbsp. curry powder

- 1 tsp. turmeric

- 1 tsp. coriander

DIRECTIONS

1. Take warm water in the bowl and soak cashews in it.

2. Now boil the water in the pot and put in all the vegetables.

3. Allow them to boil until tender.

4. Add tomatoes, olive oil, onion, garlic, and ginger to a blender.

5. Allow them to blend and make the puree.

6. Now transfer the puree to the pan and add olive oil.

7. Cook puree for 5 minutes and set it to simmer.

8. Now drain water from the cashews and add in the puree.

9. Put frozen peas in the peas and stir.

10. By continuously stirring, add in boiling vegetables.

11. Allow them to cook for 6 minutes.

12. Serve with naan or store in the freezer.

NUTRITION: Calories: 487 kcal Fat: 29 g Protein: 13 g Carbs: 51g

28. Freeze Dried Lasagna

Ready in: 2 hours 20 minutes

Servings: 12

Difficulty: Difficult

INGREDIENTS

- ¼ tsp. pepper

- ½ tsp. salt

- ½ tsp. garlic powder

- 1 ½ tsp. dried parsley

- 1 ½ tsp. dried basil

- 1 ½ tsp. dried oregano

- ½ cup parmesan

- 8 oz. cottage cheese

- ½ cup water

- ½ lb. ground sausage

- 12 pieces Barilla Oven-Ready Lasagna

- 2 eggs

- 2 cups shredded mozzarella

- 8 oz. part-skim ricotta cheese

- 24 oz. pasta sauce

- 1 lb. ground beef

DIRECTIONS

1. Allow the oven to preheat to 350 Fahrenheit.

2. Take a pan, add ground beef and sausage, and cook for a few minutes.

3. Pour pasta sauce into it and stir.

4. Add water and stir the mixture.

5. Mix ricotta, mozzarella, eggs, basil, garlic powder, pepper, cottage cheese, parmesan, oregano and basil in a bowl.

6. Take a pan and spray it with cooking spray. Spread meat sauce at the bottom and arrange three noodles, then add cheese mixture and top with meat sauce.

7. Repeat the process till the pan is stuffed to the top.

8. Add remaining mozzarella on the top.

9. Cover a piece of foil with cooking spray and the pan with the foil.

10.   Bake for an hour.

11.   Remove the pan, discard the foil and let cool.

12.   Transfer the lasagna to freeze dryer trays and place in a freeze dryer.

13.   Let the lasagna freeze dry completely.

14.   Transfer freeze-dried lasagna to airtight containers and add an oxygen absorber.

15.   Close the lids and store them in a cool, dry place.

NUTRITION: Calories: 300 kcal Fat: 21 g Protein: 21 g Carbs: 6 g

29. Beef Taco Rice Meal in A Jar

Ready in: 40 minutes

Servings: 4

Difficulty: Medium

INGREDIENTS

- 1 cup freeze-dried beef

- 1 bay leaf

- 1 cup white rice

- 1 tsp. slat

- ½ cup bell pepper, diced

- 2 tsp. beef bouillon

- 2 tbsp. minced onion

- ¼ cup tomato powder

- 2 tbsp. taco seasoning

- ½ tsp. smoked paprika

- 1 tsp. minced garlic

DIRECTIONS

1. Take a quart-size freezer bag and put in all the ingredients.

2. To settle the content in the bag, shake them well.

3. Now by following the Food Saver manual close the mouth of the bag with the Food Saver canning lid.

4. Label the bag and store it in a dry and cool location.

5. For cooking, boil the water in a pot and place the bag with an open mouth.

6. Add the boiling water to the bag and allow them to soak for 10 minutes.

7. Eat in the bag.

NUTRITION: Calories: 264 kcal Fat: 4 g Protein: 18 g Carbs: 23 g

30. Sausage and Pasta Casserole

Ready in: 50 minutes

Servings: 6

Difficulty: Medium

INGREDIENTS

- 2 cups shredded mozzarella cheese

- 6 oz. tomato paste

- 14.5 oz. diced tomatoes with garlic

- 15 oz. tomato sauce

- ½ cup white wine

- 1 cup chopped onion

- 1 lb. mild Italian sausage

- 2 tsp. olive oil

- 12 oz. dry penne pasta

DIRECTIONS

1. Allow the oven to preheat to 350 Fahrenheit.

2. Cook the pasta according to the directions given on the package.

3.   Take a large pan and heat the oil in it. Add sausage and onion and fry for a few minutes.

4.   Add wine and bring to a boil.

5.   Add tomato sauce, diced tomatoes, and tomato paste into the pan and let the mixture simmer for ten minutes.

6.   Add cooked pasta to it and mix.

7.   Take a casserole or a baking dish and coat it with cooking spray.

8.   Transfer the pasta to the dish and add mozzarella cheese on top.

9.   Bake for twenty minutes.

10.   Remove the casserole and let cool.

11.   Transfer it to freeze dryer trays and place it in a freeze dryer.

12.   Allow it to freeze dry completely.

13.   Transfer the freeze-dried casserole to an airtight container and add an oxygen absorber.

14.   Close the lid and store in a cool, dry place.

NUTRITION: Calories: 664 kcal Fat: 33.5 g Protein: 31 g Carbs: 59.2 g

31. Homestyle Chicken Noodle Casserole

Ready in: 10 minutes

Servings: 2

Difficulty: Easy

INGREDIENTS

- 1 pack freeze-dried homestyle chicken noodle casserole

- 2 cups water

DIRECTIONS

1. Tear the notch of the package of freeze-dried homestyle chicken noodle casserole.

2. Remove the oxygen absorber from its bottom to make it a bowl.

3. Add in boiling water and soak for 5 minutes.

4. Stir them well to settle all the contents in them.

5. Eat.

NUTRITION: Calories: 280 kcal Fat: 9 g Protein: 18 g Carbs: 31g

32. Organic Shepherds Meat Pie

Ready in: 5 minutes

Servings: 1

Difficulty: Easy

INGREDIENTS

- 1 pack of Mary Janes from organic shepherds Meat Pie

- ½ cup water

DIRECTIONS

1. take a pouch of Mary Janes Farm organic shepherd's meat pie.

2. Add in boiling water.

3. Stir to settle all the contents.

4. Serve.

NUTRITION: Calories: 250 kcal Fat: 6 g Protein: 15 g Carbs: 87g

33. Chicken Pho

Ready in: 20 minutes

Servings: 4

Difficulty: Easy

INGREDIENTS

- 8 cups chicken broth

- 2 Lime wedges

- 8 slices ginger

- 2/3 cup Thai basil

- 2 red chilies

- 2/3 cup fresh cilantro

- 1 tbsp. fish sauce

- 2/3 cup fresh mint

- 1 tbsp. sugar

- 12 oz. dried pho noodles

- 2 boneless chicken thighs

- 2 tbsp. oil

- ½ tsp. Salt

- ½ tsp. Pepper

DIRECTIONS

1. Boil the noodles in the boiling water in a pot and set aside.

2. Boil stock in the pot by adding fish sauce, ginger, Sugar, and chilies and set it to simmer.

3. Rub the chicken with pepper and salt.

4. Pour the oil into the pot over medium heat and sear the chicken from all sides in it by flipping.

5. Now put noodles, stock, and chicken in 4 bowls and serve.

6. Seal the noodles and chicken and place them in the freezer for storage.

NUTRITION: Calories: 557 kcal Fat: 13 g Protein: 26 g Carbs: 86g

34. Tuna Couscous Bowl

Ready in: 10 minutes

Servings: 8

Difficulty: Easy

INGREDIENTS

- 2 tsp. curry powder

- 1 tbsp. lemon juice

- 2 tbsp. sweet chili sauce

- 1 cup chopped fresh coriander

- 4 thinly sliced spring onions

- 2 cups frozen peas

- 420 g reduced-salt corn kernels

- 420 g tuna in spring water

- 1 cup boiling water

- 1 cup couscous

DIRECTIONS

1. Take a large bowl and add couscous and water to it. Cover the bowl and set aside for three minutes.

2. Add tuna, coriander, spring onions, peas, and corn in a separate bowl.

3. Take a fork and fluff couscous with it, and add chili sauce, curry powder, and lemon juice. Mix well.

4. Add salad ingredients to couscous and mix well.

5. Transfer the couscous mixture to freeze dryer trays and place in a freeze dryer.

6. Allow it to freeze dry completely.

7. Transfer the freeze-dried tuna couscous to mason jars and an oxygen absorber.

8. Close the lids and store them in a cool, dry place.

NUTRITION: Calories: 295 kcal Fat: 3 g Protein: 27.2 g Carbs: 48 g

35. Dottie's Chicken and Dumplings

Ready in: 15 minutes

Servings: 2

Difficulty: Easy

INGREDIENTS

- 1 pouch of Dottie's Chicken and Dumplings

- 1 cup boiling water

DIRECTIONS

1. Take the freeze-dried Pack It Gourmet Dottie's chicken and dumplings pouch along with all the ingredients.

2. Open its notch and remove the oxygen absorber to make it bowl.

3. Add in boiling water and allow them to soak for 5 minutes.

4. Stir them well to mix all the contents and eat.

NUTRITION: Calories: 370 kcal Fat: 6 g Protein: 44 g Carbs: 34g

36. Beef Stroganoff

Ready in: 12 minutes

Servings: 1

Difficulty: Easy

INGREDIENTS

- ½ cup noodles

- 1 cup water

- 2 tbsp. stroganoff sauce mix

- ¼ cup ground beef, dehydrated

- 1 tbsp. milk powder

- ¼ cup dried vegetables

DIRECTIONS

1.   Take a pot and put it in water.

2.   Put all the ingredients in the water except milk powder and sauce mix.

3.   Allow them to soak for 5 minutes.

4.   Boil the mixture for 2 minutes.

5.   After removing the heat, add milk powder and sauce mix by stirring to make the mixture thick.

6.   Allow them to cool and eat.

NUTRITION: Calories: 260 kcal Fat: 11 g Protein: 11 g Carbs: 29 g

37. Teriyaki Marinade

Ready in: 20 minutes

Servings: 24

Difficulty: Easy

INGREDIENTS

- 1 tsp. grated fresh ginger

- 3 tbsp. distilled white vinegar

- 1/3 cup dried onion flakes

- 1 cup water

- 2 tsp. garlic powder

- 3 tbsp. vegetable oil

- ¼ cup Worcestershire sauce

- ¾ cup white sugar

- 1 cup soy sauce

DIRECTIONS

1.   Add all the ingredients to a bowl and mix well.

2.   Transfer the marinade to freeze dryer trays.

3.   Allow it to freeze dry completely.

4.   Crumble the marinade into mason jars.

5.   Add an oxygen absorber to each jar and close the lids.

NUTRITION: Calories: 51 kcal Fat: 1.7 g Protein: 0.8 g Carbs:
8.4 g

38. Egg Fried Rice

Ready in: 30 minutes

Servings: 2

Difficulty: Easy

INGREDIENTS

- 1 tbsp. of schezwan sauce

- 3 eggs

- 3 stalks of spring onions, chopped

- 2 tbsp. olive oil

- ¼ tsp. salt

- ¼ tsp. crushed black pepper

- 1 tbsp. chopped garlic

- 1 ½ tsp. rice wine vinegar

- 1 tbsp. organic soya sauce

- 3 cups cooked rice

- ½ cup cabbage

- ½ cup red bell peppers

- ½ cup carrot

DIRECTIONS

1. Wash rice and soak them in water for thirty minutes.

2. Bring the water to a boil in a pan. Drain the rice and add them to boiling water.

3. Add ½ tsp. of salt and boil.

4. Drain the rice in a colander.

5. Take veggies and chop them and beat eggs in a bowl.

6. Heat oil in a pan and fry garlic in it.

7. Add onions and fry for two minutes.

8. Add chopped veggies and fry for two minutes.

9. Add eggs and scramble them.

10. Add soya sauce, vinegar and hot sauce and stir,

11. Add cooked rice, black pepper, and green spring onions.

12. Fry for two more minutes.

13. Turn off the heat and let it cool.

14. Transfer the rice to freeze dryer trays and place it in a freeze dryer.

15. Allow them to freeze dry completely.

16.   Transfer the freeze-dried egg fried rice to mason jars and add an oxygen absorber.

17.   Close the lids and store them in a cool, dry place.

NUTRITION: Calories: 594 kcal Fat: 21 g Protein: 18 g Carbs: 81 g

39. Freeze Dried Cheese

Ready in: 30 hours

Servings: 1 half pint jar

Difficulty: Difficult

INGREDIENTS

- 10 lbs. shredded cheese

DIRECTIONS

1. Place the cheese on Harvest Right trays and pre-freeze for some time.

2. Then place the trays in a freeze dryer and allow them to freeze dry completely.

3. Transfer the cheese to mylar bags and add an oxygen absorber to each.

4. Store in a cool and dry place.

NUTRITION: Calories: 114.5 kcal Fat: 9.4 g Protein: 6.4 g Carbs: 0.8 g

40. Greek Whole Grain Pasta Bake

Ready in: 55 minutes

Servings: 8

Difficulty: Medium

INGREDIENTS

- ¾ cup chopped fresh basil

- 1 cup shredded mozzarella cheese

- 1 tsp. dried basil

- ¼ cup thinly sliced red onion

- 10 oz. frozen chopped spinach

- 29 oz. tomato sauce

- 3 1/3 cups uncooked whole grain spiral or penne pasta

- ½ cup crumbled feta cheese

- 1tsp. dried oregano

- ¼ cup chopped green pepper

- 2 ¼ oz. sliced ripe olives

- 14 ½ no-salt-added diced tomatoes

- 4 cups cubed cooked chicken breast

DIRECTIONS

1. Allow the oven to preheat to 400 Fahrenheit.

2. Cook the pasta according to the instruction on the package.

3. Add chicken, tomato sauce, olives, tomatoes, spinach, basil, onion, oregano, and green pepper in a large bowl and mix well.

4. Add cooked pasta to the bowl and mix well.

5. Take a baking dish and coat it with cooking spray.

6. Add the mixture to the dish and add cheese on top.

7. Bake the pasta for twenty-five minutes.

8. Remove the dish and allow it to cool.

9. Transfer the paste to freeze dryer trays and place it in a freeze dryer.

10. Allow it to freeze dry completely.

11. Transfer the pasta to an airtight container and add an oxygen absorber.

12. Close the lid and store in a cool, dry place.

NUTRITION: Calories: 398 kcal Fat: 10 g Protein: 34 g Carbs: 47g

Chapter 2: Fruits and Vegetable Recipes

1. Freeze Dried Plum Bites

Ready in: 32 hours

Servings: 2 half pint jars

Difficulty: Difficult

INGREDIENTS

- ¼ cup honey

- 2 lbs. fresh plums

DIRECTIONS

1. Take fresh plums, wash them and remove stems and ends.

2. To remove the pits, cut the plums into halves.

3. Add the plums to a blender and pour honey. Blend till puree.

4. Transfer the puree to ice cube trays and place them in the freezer for some time.

5.	Place parchment paper on freeze dryer trays and the frozen plum cubes in the tray.

6.	Place the trays in the freeze dryer and allow them to freeze dry completely.

7.	Transfer them to containers and add an oxygen absorber to each jar.

8.	Close the lids and store them at room temperature out of direct sunlight.

NUTRITION: Calories: 119.7 kcal Fat: 4.8 g Protein: 3 g Carbs: 18.7 g

2. Freeze Dried Tomatoes

Ready in: 16 hours and 10 minutes

Servings: 6

Difficulty: Difficult

INGREDIENTS

- 6 cups tomatoes

DIRECTIONS

1. Wash the tomatoes and slice them.

2. Arrange them on freeze dryer trays and place the trays in a freeze dryer.

3. Allow them to freeze dry completely.

4. Transfer the freeze-dried tomatoes to mason jars and add an oxygen absorber.

5. Close the lids and store them in a cool, dry place.

NUTRITION: Calories: 29.6 kcal Fat: 0.33 g Protein: 145 g Carbs: 6.4 g

3. Freeze Dried Beans

Ready in: 13 hours

Servings: 16

Difficulty: Difficult

INGREDIENTS

- 8 tbsp. salt

- 20 cups water

- 1 lb. dried black beans

DIRECTIONS

1. Take a large bowl and add water and beans to it. Set them aside for one hour.

2. Add the beans to a large pot and add water and salt. Bring to a boil and let simmer for an hour.

3. Drain the beans in a colander.

4. Let them dry completely.

5.   Then place them on freeze dryer trays and place them in a
        freeze dryer.

6.   Allow them to freeze dry completely.

7.   Transfer the freeze-dried beans to mason jars and add an
        oxygen absorber to each.

8.   Close the lids and store them in a cool, dry place.

NUTRITION: Calories: 96 kcal Fat: 0 g Protein: 6 g Carbs: 17 g

4. Freeze Dried Spinach

Ready in: 10 minutes

Servings: 8

Difficulty: Easy

INGREDIENTS

- 16 oz. washed and dried spinach

DIRECTIONS

1. Place spinach on freeze dryer trays and put the trays in a freeze dryer.

2. Allow it to freeze dry completely.

3. Transfer the freeze-dried spinach to zip lock bags and add an oxygen absorber to each.

4. Seal the bags and store them in a cool, dry place.

NUTRITION: Calories: 13 kcal Fat: 1 g Protein: 2 g Carbs: 2 g

5. Freeze Dried Corn

Ready in: 42 hours

Servings: 30

Difficulty: Difficult

INGREDIENTS

- 10 lb. sweet corn

DIRECTIONS

1. Shuck the corn and cut the corn off the cob. Blanch for three minutes.

2. Add blanched corn to an ice-water bath.

3. Take freeze dryer trays and cover with parchment paper.

4. Drain the corns and place them in freeze-dryer trays.

5. Place the trays in a freeze-dryer.

6. Allow the corn to freeze dry completely.

7. Transfer the corn to a mylar bag and add an oxygen absorber.

8. Seal the bag and store it in a cool, dry place.

NUTRITION: Calories: 130 kcal Fat: 2 g Protein: 4.9 g Carbs: 28.3 g

6. Freeze-Dried Cinnamon Apples

Ready in: 12 hours 20 minutes

Servings: 8

Difficulty: Difficult

INGREDIENTS

- 1 tsp. vanilla extract

- ½ tsp. nutmeg

- 2 tsp. cinnamon

- 2 tbsp. sugar

- 1 lemon

- 5 apples

DIRECTIONS

1. Take apples, core, and slice them into rings.

2. Add nutmeg, cinnamon, vanilla extract, lemon juice and sugar to a bowl and mix.

3. Add apple rings and cinnamon mixture to a zip lock bag and toss to coat apples with cinnamon.

4.   Arrange apple slices on freeze dryer trays and place them in a freeze dryer.

5.   Allow them to freeze dry completely.

6.   Transfer the apple slices to mason jars and add oxygen absorbers.

7.   Close the lids and store them in a cool, dry place.

NUTRITION: Calories: 78 kcal Fat: 1 g Protein: 1 g Carbs: 20 g

7. Freeze-Dried Strawberries

Ready in: 10 hours

Servings: 5

Difficulty: Difficult

INGREDIENTS

- 4 lbs. Strawberries

DIRECTIONS

1. Rinse strawberries and dry with a paper towel.

2. Cut each strawberry into 5 slices.

3. Put the sliced strawberries on the freeze-dryer tray.

4. Place the tray in the freeze dryer and turn it on.

5. Freeze dryer runs until strawberries are completely dried.

6. After removing them from the dryer, transfer strawberries into an airtight container and store them in the freezer.

NUTRITION: Calories: 44.67 kcal Fat: 0.02 g Protein: 0.94 g Carbs: 10.72 g

8. Freeze Dried Raspberries

Ready in: 24 hours

Servings: 40

Difficulty: Difficult

INGREDIENTS

- 10 lb. Raspberries

DIRECTIONS

1. Wash the raspberries and remove the stem from them.

2. Pat dry raspberries with a paper towel.

3. Place the raspberries in the freeze-dryer tray.

4. Run the freeze dryer until the raspberries completely dry.

5. Remove raspberries from the dryer and put them in the airtight container.

6. Store in the freezer.

NUTRITION: Calories: 58.97 kcal Fat: 0.02 g Protein: 1.36 g Carbs: 13.49 g

9. Freeze Dried Peaches

Ready in: 24 hour

Servings: 10

Difficulty: Difficult

INGREDIENTS

- 4 lb. peaches

DIRECTIONS

1. Wash peaches and pat dry with a paper towel.

2. Slice peaches into four.

3. Put the peach slices in the freeze-dryer tray.

4. Run the freeze-dryer machine until the peaches are fully dried.

5. Remove the peaches from the freeze dryer tray and sealed in the airtight container.

6. Place in the refrigerator.

NUTRITION: Calories: 70 kcal Fat: 0.00 g Protein: 1 g Carbs: 18 g

10. Freeze Dried Pineapple

Ready in: 12 hour

Servings: 7

Difficulty: Difficult

INGREDIENTS

- 4 lb. pineapple

DIRECTIONS

1. Cut the pineapple into pieces.

2. Place the pieces of pineapple in the freeze-dryer tray.

3. Run the freeze-dryer until the pineapple is completely dry.

4. Seal in the airtight container and place in the freezer.
   NUTRITION: Calories: 5 kcal Fat: 0 g Protein: 0 g Carbs:
   6 g

11. Freeze Dried Bananas

Ready in: 24 hours

Servings: 6

Difficulty: Difficult

INGREDIENTS

- 10 lb. bananas

DIRECTIONS

1. Peel bananas and cut them into pieces.

2. Place the pieces of bananas in the tray of the freeze dryer.

3. Run the dryer until the bananas are fully dried.

4. Seal in the airtight container and place in the freezer.

NUTRITION: Calories: 137.5 kcal Fat: 0.5 g Protein: 1.65 g Carbs: 34.47 g

12. Freeze Dried Blackberries

Ready in: 12 hours

Servings: 4

Difficulty: Difficult

INGREDIENTS

- 2 lbs. blackberries

DIRECTIONS

1. Wash blackberries with fresh water.

2. As blackberries are so soft, carefully pat dry with a towel.

3. Put in the freeze dryer tray.

4. Run the freeze-dryer to dry completely.

5. After removing from the dryer, transfer to the container and store in the freezer.

NUTRITION: Calories: 48 kcal Fat: 0 g Protein: 1 g Carbs: 10 g

13. Freeze Dried Blueberries

Ready in: 16 hours

Servings: 6

Difficulty: Difficult

INGREDIENTS

- 10 lbs. Blueberries

DIRECTIONS

1. Firstly, wash the blueberries and pat dry with a paper towel.

2. Now place the blueberries in the tray.

3. Put the tray in the Harvest right freeze dryer.

4. Run the dryer to dry the blueberries.

5. Once drying is done, transfer into the airtight container and store in the freezer.

NUTRITION: Calories: 40 kcal Fat: 0 g Protein: 0 g Carbs: 8 g

14. Freeze Dried Mushrooms

Ready in: 15 hours

Servings: 6

Difficulty: Difficult

INGREDIENTS

- 5lbs. Mushrooms

DIRECTIONS

1. Wash mushrooms with fresh water and dry with a paper towel.

2. Arrange in the tray.

3. Put the tray in the freeze dryer.

4. Run the machine for drying.

5. After drying, seal in the container and store in the freezer.
   NUTRITION: Calories: 5 kcal Fat: 0 g Protein: 1 g Carbs:
   1 g

15. Freeze Dried Onions

Ready in: 12 hours

Servings: 9

Difficulty: Difficult

INGREDIENTS

- 2 lbs. onions

DIRECTIONS

1. Take onions and peel them off.

2. Sliced the onions in pieces of the desired size.

3. Place the onion in the tray in one layer.

4. Fix the tray in the freeze dryer.

5. Run freeze dryer machine for complete drying.

6. Once done, transfer the dried onions into the sealed bag and store them in the freezer.

NUTRITION: Calories: 44 kcal Fat: 0 g Protein: 1 g Carbs: 10 g

16. Freeze Dried Carrots

Ready in: 16 hours

Servings: 8

Difficulty: Difficult

INGREDIENTS

- 5 lbs. carrots

- 2 cups water

DIRECTIONS

1. Wash the carrots with fresh water and peel them off.

2. Cut carrots into coin-size pieces.

3. Boil the water in a pot on medium heat.

4. Put in carrots and allow them to boil for 5 to 3 minutes.

5. After removing the pot, arrange the carrot pieces in the freeze-dryer tray.

6. Run the freeze-dryer to dry.

7. After removing the dryer, seal the bag and store it in the freezer.

NUTRITION: Calories: 186 kcal Fat: 1 g Protein: 4 g Carbs: 43 g

17. Freeze Dried Peas

Ready in: 10 hours

Servings: 5

Difficulty: Difficult

INGREDIENTS

- 1 cup Water

- 1 kg peas

DIRECTIONS

1.	Take peas and take kernels from them by shelling them.

2.	Now boil the water in the pot and put in the peas.

3.	Allow them to boil for 5 minutes.

4.	After removing from the pot, spread peas in the tray and allow them to cool.

5.	Then place the tray in the freeze dryer.

6.	Run the machine to dry peas.

7.	After that, transfer peas to the sealed bag and place them in the freezer.

NUTRITION: Calories: 825 kcal Fat: 4 g Protein: 54 g Carbs: 149g

18. Freeze Dried Asparagus

Ready in: 12 hours

Servings: 5

Difficulty: Difficult

INGREDIENTS

- 2 cups Water

- 4 lbs. Asparagus

DIRECTIONS

1. Firstly, wash the asparagus and then cut it into pieces.

2. Pat dry pieces of asparagus with a paper towel.

3. Boil the water in the pot and put in citric acid.

4. Add cut pieces of asparagus to the water and allow them to boil for 5 minutes.

5. Arrange the asparagus in the tray after removing it from the water.

6. Allow them to cool and place them in the freeze dryer.

7. Run the dryer, and after drying, transfer to the sealed bag.

8. Store in the freezer.

NUTRITION: Calories: 20 kcal Fat: 0 g Protein: 4 g Carbs: 4 g

19. Freeze-Dried Pumpkin

Ready in: 15 hours

Servings: 6

Difficulty: Difficult

INGREDIENTS

- 2 cups Water

- 7 lbs. pumpkin

DIRECTIONS

1. Take the pumpkin and peel them off.

2. Cut the pumpkin into cubes.

3. Now boil the water in a pot and add cubes of pumpkin.

4. Boil pumpkin for 10 minutes.

5. Now arrange them in the tray and allow them to cool.

6. Fix the tray in the freeze dryer.

7. Run the dryer to dry the pumpkin completely.

8. After that, transfer pumpkin cubes into the sealed bag and freeze.

NUTRITION: Calories: 35 kcal Fat: 0 g Protein: 0 g Carbs: 8 g

20. Apple Crisp

Ready in: 1 hour 20 minutes

Servings: 12

Difficulty: Difficult

INGREDIENTS

- ½ cup melted butter

- ¼ tsp. baking soda

- ¼ tsp. baking powder

- 1 cup packed brown sugar

- 1 cup all-purpose flour

- 1 cup quick-cooking oats

- ½ cup water

- 1 tsp. ground cinnamon

- 1 tbsp. all-purpose flour

- 1 cup white sugar

- 10 cups all-purpose apples, peeled, cored, and sliced

DIRECTIONS

1.   Allow the oven to preheat to 350 Fahrenheit.

2.   Add sliced apples to a pan, sugar, flour and cinnamon, and mix well.

3.   Add water evenly.

4.   Add butter, baking soda, oats, brown sugar, flour and baking powder to a bowl and mix well.

5.   Sprinkle the mixture over the apple mixture.

6.   Bake for forty-five minutes.

7.   Transfer the apple crisp to freeze dryer trays and place in a freeze dryer.

8.   Allow them to freeze dry completely.

9.   Transfer them to mason jars and add an oxygen absorber.

10. Close the lids and store them in a cool, dry place.

NUTRITION: Calories: 316 kcal Fat: 8.4 g Protein: 2.4 g Carbs: 60.5 g

21. Freeze-Dried Raspberry Jam

Ready in: 50 minutes

Servings: Two 8-oz. mason jars

Difficulty: Medium

INGREDIENTS

- 1 pinch Wildly Organic Himalayan Pink Salt

- 1 cup water

- 1 cup raspberries

- 3 tbsp. low sugar pectin

- ¼ cup Wildly Organic Coconut Syrup

DIRECTIONS

1. Take 2 8 oz. Mason jars and sterilize them.

2. Take a saucepan and add raspberries, coconut syrup, water, and pink salt.

3. Let the mixture simmer for five minutes.

4. Turn off the heat, add pectin and stir.

5. Transfer the jam to freeze dryer trays and place them in a freeze dryer.

6. Allow the jam to freeze dry completely.

7.   Transfer the jam to mason jars and add an oxygen absorber to each jar.

8.   Close the lids and store them in a cool, dry place.

NUTRITION: Calories: 39 kcal Fat: 0 g Protein: 0 g Carbs: 0 g

22. Peach Cobbler

Ready in: 3 minutes

Servings: 1

Difficulty: Easy

INGREDIENTS

- 6 bags freeze dried peaches

- Salt as required

- 3tbsp. Brown sugar

- ¼ tsp. baking powder

- 1 tbsp. Butter

- ¼ tsp. vanilla extract

- 2 tbsp. all-purpose flour

- 1 tbsp. granulated sugar

- 2 tbsp. milk

DIRECTIONS

1. Take a bowl and soak the peaches in water in it.

2.   Mix peaches with cinnamon and brown sugar and microwave for thirty seconds.

3.   Place the butter over the peaches and microwave for more than 30 seconds until melted and completely incorporated into the peaches.

4.   Take another bowl and mix in all the remaining ingredients.

5.   Now pour the flour over the peach mixture and cook for one more minute.

6.   Allow it to cool and store in the container.

7.   Place in the freezer.

NUTRITION: Calories: 100 kcal Fat: 12 g Protein: 23 g Carbs: 34 g

23. Strawberry Yogurt

Ready in: 5 minutes

Servings: 1

Difficulty: Easy

INGREDIENTS

- ½ cup plain Greek yogurt

- 1 ½ cup fresh strawberries

- ½ cup whipped cream

- 2 tbsp. honey

DIRECTIONS

1. Take a small bowl and mash the strawberries using a muddler.

2. Add honey and yogurt and mix well.

3. Transfer the strawberry yogurt to freeze dryer trays and add whipped crema on top.

4. Allow it to freeze dry completely.

5. Transfer the yogurt to a jar.

6. Add an oxygen absorber and close the lid.

7. Store in a cool and dry place.

NUTRITION: Calories: 182 kcal Fat: 1 g Protein: 12 g Carbs: 34g

24. Cuban Coconut Rice and Black Beans

Ready in: 5 minutes

Servings: 1

Difficulty: Easy

INGREDIENTS

- 1 pack backpacker's pantry Cuban coconut rice and black beans

- 1/2 cup water

DIRECTIONS

1. Take a freeze-dried pouch of Cuban coconut rice and black beans and make it in a bowl.

2. Boil water and pour into the pouch.

3. Allow them to soak for 5 minutes.

4. Stir to mix and eat.

NUTRITION: Calories: 300 kcal Fat: 2 g Protein: 12 g Carbs: 60g

Chapter 3: Breakfast and Dessert Recipes

1. Peanut Butter Choc Chip Banana Bread

Ready in: 1 hour 55 minutes

Servings: 12

Difficulty: Difficult

INGREDIENTS

- ¾ cup semi-sweet chocolate chips

- 1 large egg

- ¾ cup brown sugar

- 2 mashed ripe bananas

- ½ tsp. baking soda

- 1 cup whole wheat flour

- 1 tbsp. canola oil

- ¼ cup plain fat-free yogurt

- 1/3 cup unsweetened crunchy peanut butter

- ¼ tsp. salt

- 1 tsp. baking powder

- Cooking spray

DIRECTIONS

1   Allow the oven to preheat at 330 Fahrenheit.

2.   Take a loaf pan and coat it with cooking spray.

3.   Add flour, baking powder, salt and soda to a large bowl and mix well.

4.   Mix mashed bananas, brown sugar, canola oil, peanut butter, egg, and yogurt in another bowl.

5.   Transfer the banana mixture to the flour mixture and mix well.

6.   Add chocolate chips and stir.

7.   Transfer the batter to the loaf pan and place it in the oven.

8.   Bake the bread for about fifty minutes.

9.   Let the bread cool down and cut into slices.

10.   Place the bread slices on a freeze dryer tray and place them in a freeze dryer.

11.   Allow the bread slices to freeze dry completely.

12.   Place the bread slices in an airtight container along with an oxygen absorber.

13.   Close the lid and store in a cool, dry place.

NUTRITION: Calories: 201 kcal Fat: 8.7 g Protein: 4.4 g Carbs:29

2. Salted Caramel Blondies

Ready in: 1 hour 20 minutes

Servings: 20

Difficulty: Difficult

INGREDIENTS

- 100 g light brown muscovado sugar

- 3 eggs

- Pinch of sea salt

- 200 g chopped white chocolate

- 300 g plain flour

- 200 g light brown soft sugar

- 397 g carnation caramel

- 150 g unsalted butter

DIRECTIONS

1. Allow the oven to preheat.

2. Take a pan and add butter, half of the white chocolate, 100 g caramel and sugar to it and heat till the mixture melts completely. Turn off the heat.

3.   In a separate bowl, add the remaining caramel and salt and mix.

4.   Add eggs to the pan containing the melted mixture and whisk.

5.   Add flour and mix well, so no lumps remain.

6   Add remaining white chocolate and stir.

7.   Take a cake tin line with baking paper and pour half the blondie batter. Add half of the salted caramel on top, and then pour the rest of the blondie batter on top.

8.   Drizzle the remaining salted caramel and marble the caramel and blondie mixture using a skewer.

9.   Place the cake tin in the oven and bake for sixty minutes.

10.   Remove the tin and allow it to cool.

11.   Cut the cake into 20 pieces and place them on freeze dryer trays.

12.   Place the trays in a freeze-dryer and allow them to freeze dry completely.

13.   Transfer the blondies to airtight containers and add oxygen absorbers.

14.   Close the lids and store them in a cool, dry place away from direct sunlight.

NUTRITION: Calories: 298 kcal Fat: 11.4 g Protein: 10.8 g Carbs: 9.7g

3. Maple Muffins

Ready in: 30 minutes

Servings: 16

Difficulty: Easy

INGREDIENTS

- ½ tsp. vanilla extract

- ¼ cup sour cream

- ½ cup melted butter

- ½ tsp. salt

- ½ cup packed brown sugar

- 1 large egg

- ½ cup maple syrup

- ¾ cup 2% milk

- 2 tsp. baking powder

- 2 cups all-purpose flour

Topping

- 2 tbsp. cold butter

- ½ tsp. ground cinnamon

- 2 tbsp. chopped nuts

- 3 tbsp. sugar

- 3 tbsp. all-purpose flour

DIRECTIONS

1. Allow the oven to preheat to 400 Fahrenheit.

2. Add flour, brown sugar, salt, and baking powder to a bowl and mix well.

3. Mix milk, syrup, vanilla, butter, egg, and sour cream in a separate bowl. Transfer the mixture to another bowl containing flour mixture and mix well.

4. Take muffin cups lined with parchment paper and fill about two third of the cups with batter.

5. Mix flour, sugar, cinnamon, nut and butter in a separate bowl.

6. Sprinkle the mixture over the batter in muffin cups.

7. Bake them for twenty minutes and let them cool.

8.   Transfer the muffins to freeze dryer trays and place them in a freeze dryer.

9.   Allow them to freeze dry completely.

10.   Transfer them to airtight containers and add an oxygen absorber.

11.   Close the lids and store them in a cool, dry place.

NUTRITION: Calories: 212 kcal Fat: 9 g Protein: 3 g Carbs: 30g

4. Strawberry Lemonade Deep Dish pie

Ready in: 3 hours 15

minutes Servings: 6

Difficulty: Difficult

INGREDIENTS

- **Graham Cracker Crust**

- 3 tbsp. sugar

- 8 tbsp. salted butter

- 2 cups crushed graham crackers

- **Lemonade Pie Filling**

- 20 sliced strawberries

- ½ cup fresh lemon juice

- 5 large egg yolks

- ¼ tsp. vanilla extract

- 14 oz. sweetened condensed milk

- **Meringue Topping**

- 5 tbsp. sugar

- 5 large egg whites

DIRECTIONS

1. Take a bowl and separate egg whites from egg yolks.

2. Beat the egg whites along with sugar to make meringue and set aside.

3. Beat the egg yolks using a fork.

4. Cut lemons and squeeze to get lemon juice.

5. Add the juice to egg yolks along with condensed milk and mix.

6. Add vanilla and whisk.

7. Prepare the crust by mixing graham crackers, sugar, and melted butter in a bowl.

8. Allow the oven to preheat to 325 degrees.

9. Transfer the mixture from the bowl to a deep pie dish and press the crust on the bottom and sides.

10. Place the dish in the oven and bake for fifteen minutes.

11. Remove the dish from the oven and set the oven to 350 degrees.

12. Pour the pie filling onto the crust and bake for twelve more minutes.

13. Place the pie in the refrigerator to cool.

14.   Remove the pie and place sliced strawberries on top.

15.   Add meringue on top.

16.   Transfer the pie to freeze dryer trays and place in a freeze dryer.

17.   Allow the pie to freeze dry completely.

18.   Transfer the pie to airtight containers and add an oxygen absorber.

19.   Cover the containers and store them in a cool, dry place. NUTRITION: Calories: 495 kcal Fat: 13 g Protein: 13 g Carbs: 84 g

5. Ginger and Lemon Cake

Ready in: 60 minutes

Servings: 14

Difficulty: Medium

INGREDIENTS

For the sponge

- 1 egg

- 140 g dark brown sugar

- 2 tsp. mixed spice

- 1 tsp. bicarbonate of soda

- 140 g golden syrup

- 140 g butter

- 300 ml whole milk

- 1 tsp. ground cinnamon

- 4 tsp. ground ginger

- 300 g self-rising flour

- 140 g black treacle

For lemon curd filling

- 2 diced stem ginger

- 160 g lemon curd

For creamy icing

- 2 tbsp. icing sugar

- 200 ml double cream

- 100 g cream cheese

- 4 tbsp. syrup from stem ginger jar

DIRECTIONS

1. Allow the oven to preheat.

2. Heat butter in a pan and add black treacle and golden syrup.

3. Mix self-rising flour, ground ginger, bicarbonate of soda, cinnamon, mixed spice and dark brown sugar in a separate bowl.

4. Add butter mixture to the flour mixture in the bowl and mix well.

5. Add eggs and milk to a separate bowl and whisk together.

6. Transfer them to the mixture in the large bowl and mix well.

7. Transfer the mixture to tins and bake for thirty minutes.

8.   Add lemon curd and diced ginger to a bowl and mix to prepare the filling.

9.   Prepare the icing by beating ginger syrup, cream cheese, icing sugar and double cream and mix well.

10.   Take one-half of the sponge cake and add filling at the bottom. Add icing on top and cover with the other half of the sponge.

11.   Transfer the cake to a freeze-drying tray and place it in a freeze-dryer.

12.   Allow it to freeze dry completely.

13.   Transfer the cake to an airtight container and add an oxygen absorber.

14.   Close the lids and store them in a cool, dry place.

NUTRITION: Calories: 386 kcal Fat: 18 g Protein: 5 g Carbs: 50g

6. Key Lime Tarts

Ready in: 1 hour and 15 minutes

Servings: 8

Difficulty: Difficult

INGREDIENTS

- ¼ Coconut Pastry

- ¼ tsp. coconut flavoring

- 1 large egg yolk

- 125 g unsalted butter

- 40 g icing sugar

- 25 g desiccated coconut, toasted

- 200 g plain flour

Filling

- 2 limes, zested

- 397 g tin condensed milk

- 150 ml lime juice

- 3 large egg yolks

Topping

- 1 lime, zested

- 300 ml double cream

DIRECTIONS

1. Prepare the pastry by mixing flour, coconut, salt, and icing sugar in a blender and blending.

2. Add butter and blend some more.

3. Add egg yolk, ice cold water and coconut flavoring and again blend.

4. Transfer the mixture to the workstation and kneed it gently to prepare the dough.

5. Make a thick sausage shape from the dough and place them in the refrigerator for two hours to chill.

6. Remove the pastry from the fridge and cut it into eight rounds.

7. Roll each round and line it over tart tins; trim the excess.

8. Place them in the refrigerator again to chill.

9. Line each tart shell with parchment paper and fill with baking beans.

10.   Bake for fifteen minutes.

11.   Remove the baking beans with the baking paper and bake the shells for another five minutes.

12.   Prepare the filling by whisking egg yolks and lime zest together.

13.   Add lime juice and condensed milk and whisk some more.

14.   Pour the filling into tart shells and bake for fifteen minutes.

15.   Top with whipped cream and lemon zest.

16.   Transfer them to freeze dryer trays and place them in a freeze dryer.

17.   Allow them to freeze dry completely.

18.   Transfer them to an airtight container and add an oxygen absorber.

19.   Close the lid and store in a cool, dry place.

NUTRITION: Calories: 623 kcal Fat: 42.1 g Protein: 8.5 g Carbs: 51.7 g

7. Raspberry Marshmallow Crème Pie

Ready in: 30 minutes

Servings: 8

Difficulty: Easy

INGREDIENTS

Crust

- 1/3 cup melted butter

- 3 tbsp. sugar

- 1 ½ cups graham cracker crumbs

Filling

- 1 cups fresh raspberries

- A few drops of red food coloring

- 2/3 cup heavy whipping cream

- 1/3 cup milk

- 24 large marshmallows

DIRECTIONS

1. Add the ingredients for the crust to a bowl and mix.

2. Press the crust mix to the bottom of a pan and place it in the freezer for some time.

3. In the meantime, take a saucepan, add milk and marshmallows, and heat.

4. Add cream and food coloring and stir.

5. Pour half the mixture on top of the crust and add strawberries, then add the remaining mixture on top.

6. Finish with raspberries on top and place in the refrigerator for some time.

7. Transfer the pie to freeze dryer trays and place in a freeze dryer.

8. Allow it to freeze dry completely.

9. Transfer it to an airtight container and add an oxygen absorber.

10. Close the lid and store in a cool, dry place.

NUTRITION: Calories: 310 kcal Fat: 17 g Protein: 3 g Carbs: 39g

8. Backpacker's Chocolate and Berry Bark

Ready in: 20 minutes

Servings: 18

Difficulty: Easy

INGREDIENTS

- ¼ cup soy nuts

- ¼ cup pistachios

- 16 oz. dark chocolate

- 1/3 cup sliced almonds

- 6 oz. Driscoll's Blueberries

DIRECTIONS

1. Take a baking sheet and line it with parchment paper.

2. Add sliced almonds and pistachios to the pan and cook for five minutes.

3. Once they are toasted, turn off the heat and set them aside.

4. Add dark chocolate to a bowl and melt it by placing it in the microwave.

5.   Pour the chocolate over parchment paper and spread it evenly.

6.   Add blueberries and toasted almonds, and pistachios on top of the chocolate.

7.   Press them gently into the chocolate.

8.   Cover the baking sheet with cling foil and place in the refrigerator for an hour.

9.   Remove the baking sheet and break the bark into multiple pieces.

10.   Transfer the bark to freeze dryer trays and place it in a freeze dryer.

11.   Allow it to freeze dry completely.

12.   Transfer it to airtight jars and add an oxygen absorber.

13.   Close the lids and store them in a cool and dry place.

NUTRITION: Calories: 161.87 kcal Fat: 9.52 g Protein: 2.40 g Carbs: 19.76g

9. Crème Brulee

Ready in: 1 hour 10 minutes

Servings: 4

Difficulty: Difficult

INGREDIENTS

- 50 g golden caster sugar

- 5 large egg yolks

- 1 vanilla pod

- 100 ml whole milk

- 2 cartons of double cream

DIRECTIONS

1. Allow the oven to preheat.

2. Take a large pan and add double cream and milk to it.

3. Slice the vanilla pot and add seeds to the pan containing milk and cream.

4. Bring the mixture to a boil.

5. Turn off the heat.

6. Add egg yolks and sugar to a bowl and whisk them together.

7. Add the hot cream mixture to beaten eggs and sugar and whisk some more.

8. Take a large bowl and strain the mixture through a sieve into the bowl.

9. Pour the cream mixture into ramekins and put them in the oven. Cover the ramekins with a baking sheet.

10. Bake for thirty minutes.

11. Transfer the ramekins to the refrigerator to let them cool.

12. Sprinkle the Brulee with sugar.

13. Transfer the crème Brulee to freeze dryer trays and place in a freeze dryer.

14. Allow them to freeze dry completely.

15. Transfer them to an airtight container and add an oxygen absorber.

16. Close the lid and store in a cool, dry place.

NUTRITION: Calories: 620 kcal Fat: 59 g Protein: 6 g Carbs: 17g

10. Bliss Balls

Ready in: 10 minutes

Servings: 20

Difficulty: Easy

INGREDIENTS

- ½ cup desiccated coconut

- 2 tbsp. cocoa powder

- 1 tsp. ground cinnamon

- 2 tbsp. ground flax seeds

- ½ cup dried apricots

- 200 g pitted and chopped dates

- ½ cup walnuts

- 1 cup almonds

DIRECTIONS

1. Add nuts, dates, apricots, flax seeds, cocoa and cinnamon to a food processor and blend them.

2. Transfer the mixture to a bowl and make 20 balls.

3. Roll the balls in coconut to coat them evenly.

4. Place them in the refrigerator to chill.

5. Arrange the balls on a freeze dryer tray and place them in a freeze dryer.

6. Allow them to freeze dry completely.

7. Transfer them to mason jars and add oxygen absorbers.

8. Close the lids and store them in a cool, dry place.

NUTRITION: Calories: 598 kcal Fat: 9 g Protein: 3 g Carbs: 11 g

11. Raspberry Cocoa Energy Balls

Ready in: 30 minutes

Servings: 12

Difficulty: Easy

INGREDIENTS

- 2 cups shredded coconut

- 1 pinch cardamom

- ½ cup crushed raspberries

- 1/8 tsp. sea salt

- 3 tbsp. cocoa powder

- 1 tsp. vanilla extract

- 1 1/3 cup pitted Medjool dates

- ½ tbsp. coconut oil

- 1 cup shredded coconut

- 1 cup raw walnuts

DIRECTIONS

1.   Add coconut and walnuts to a food processor and blend them.

2.   Add ingredients except for raspberries and coconut for garnishing and blend them for two minutes.

3.   Prepare 12 balls from the mixture.

4.   Roll them in crushed raspberries and coconut to coat them evenly.

5.   Place them in the refrigerator to chill.

6.   Arrange the balls on a freeze dryer tray and place them in a freeze dryer.

7.   Allow them to freeze dry completely.

8.   Transfer them to a mason jar and add an oxygen absorber.

9.   Close the lid and store them in a cool, dry place.

NUTRITION: Calories: 155 kcal Fat: 0 g Protein: 2 g Carbs: 18g

12. Mocha Peanut Butter and Banana Smoothie

Ready in: 5 minutes

Servings: 2

Difficulty: Easy

INGREDIENTS

- ½ cup unsweetened almonds

- 5 Ice cubes

- ½ cup brewed coffee

- 1 tbsp. chia seeds

- 1/3 frozen banana

- 1 tbsp. peanut butter

DIRECTIONS

1. Take a blender and put in all the ingredients.

2. Allow them to blend until smooth.

3. Put in ice cubes and serve.

NUTRITION: Calories: 108 kcal Fat: 7 g Protein: 4 g Carbs: 10g

13. Peanut Butter Cheerio Cereal Bars

Ready in: 4 hours 5 minutes

Servings: 16

Difficulty: Difficult

INGREDIENTS

- 20 g roughly chopped strawberries

- 1/3 cup honey

- 2/3 cups smooth peanut butter

- 1 cup rolled oats

- 2 cups cheerios

DIRECTIONS

1. Take a large pan and line it with parchment paper.

2. Add cheerios and oats to a bowl and mix.

3. Mix peanut butter and honey separately and pour them over cheerios and oats. Mix well.

4. Add chopped strawberries and stir.

5. Transfer the mixture to the parchment-lined pan and place in the refrigerator for a few hours.

6.   Remove the pan and break it into smaller pieces.

7.   Transfer the bars to freeze dryer trays and place them in a freeze dryer.

8.   Allow them to freeze dry completely.

9.   Transfer the bars to jars and add oxygen absorbers.

10.   Close the lids and store them in a cool, dry place.
        NUTRITION: Calories: 119 kcal Fat: 6 g Protein: 3 g Carbs: 15g

14. No-Churn Freeze Dried Fruit Ice Cream

Ready in: 8 hours 30 minutes

Servings: 8

Difficulty: Difficult

INGREDIENTS

- ½ oz. complementary spirit such as Smith & Cross Jamaica Rum

- 1/8 tsp. coriander

- 2 ¼ oz. dried blueberries, ground to a fine powder

- 12 oz. heavy cream

- ½ tsp. cream of tartar

- ¼ tsp. Diamond Crystal kosher salt

- 5 ¾ oz. sugar

- 5 oz. egg whites

DIRECTIONS

1. Take a large pot. Fill it with water to a few inches and bring it to a boil.

2. Take a piece of foil, crumple it to form a ring and place it at the bottom of the pot to act as a booster seat.

3.   Add egg whites, salt, sugar, and cream of tartar to a stand mixer bowl and mix.

4.   Place the bowl over the foil ring in the water bath.

5.   Stir for about five minutes till the temperature reaches 165 Fahrenheit.

6.   Remove the bowl and whip it for five minutes to prepare the meringue.

7.   Add blueberries, rum, coriander and heavy cream to a separate bowl and whip again till it stiffens.

8.   Mix the whipped cream and meringue, and add salt or spices if needed.

9.   Scrape the ice cream into a container and cover it with foil.

10.   Place it in the freezer till it is firm.

11.   Transfer it to freeze-dryer trays and place it in a freeze-dryer.

12.   Allow it to freeze dry completely.

13.   Transfer it to an airtight container and add an oxygen absorber.

14.   Close the lid and store in a cool, dry place.

NUTRITION: Calories: 243 kcal Fat: 15 g Protein: 3 g Carbs: 23g

15. Oatmeal Freeze Dried Cookies

Ready in: 1 day, 20 hours, and 10 minutes

Servings: 20

Difficulty: Difficult

INGREDIENTS

- 1 cup rolled oats

- 1 tsp. cinnamon

- ¼ tsp. salt

- 1 ½ tsp. butter

- 2 tbsp. sweetener

- 2 cups milk

- 5 medium apples

DIRECTIONS

1. Take apples, wash them, and chop them into thin slices.

2. Arrange them at the bottom of the crockpot.

3. Add remaining ingredients and cook on low heat for eight hours.

4.   Transfer it to freeze dryer trays and place it in a freeze dryer.

5.   Allow the mix to freeze-dry completely.

6.   Transfer it to an airtight container and add an oxygen absorber.

7.   Close the lid and store in a cool, dry place.

NUTRITION: Calories: 167 kcal Fat: 6.4 g Protein: 2.2 g Carbs: 25.7g

16. Date and Almond Bliss Balls

Ready in: 20 minutes

Servings: 16

Difficulty: Easy

INGREDIENTS

- ¼ tsp. salt

- 1 tsp. vanilla extract

- 1 cup Medjool dates, pitted

- ½ cup shredded coconut

- 1 ½ cup raw almonds

DIRECTIONS

1. Add almonds, shredded coconut, vanilla extract, Medjool dates and salt to a food processor and process for a few minutes.

2. Transfer the dough to a bowl and make 16 balls.

3. Roll them in coconut to coat them evenly.

4. Place them in the refrigerator for some time to chill.

5.   Arrange them on a freeze drier tray and place them in a freeze dryer.

6.   Allow them to freeze dry completely.

7.   Transfer them to a mason jar and add an oxygen absorber.

8.   Close the lid and store in a cool, dry place.

NUTRITION: Calories: 138 kcal Fat: 7 g Protein: 3 g Carbs: 19.5g

17. Banana Pudding

Ready in: 10 minutes

Servings: 1

Difficulty: Easy

INGREDIENTS

- 1 cup water

- ¾ cup banana leather

DIRECTIONS

1. Take cold water, put in the banana leather, and mix them well by stirring continuously.

2. Serve and enjoy.

NUTRITION: Calories: 40 kcal Fat: 0 g Protein: 0 g Carbs: 9 g

18. Santa Fe Corn Pudding

Ready in: 10 minutes

Servings: 1

Difficulty: Easy

INGREDIENTS

- 1 pack of Santa Fe Corn Pudding

- 2 cup water

DIRECTIONS

1. Take a pouch of Santa Fe corn pudding and all its ingredients.

2. Boil water in the pot.

3. Put boiling water in the pouch and soak for 5 minutes.

4. Stir to mix all the content well.

5. Serve.

NUTRITION: Calories: 480 kcal Fat: 17 g Protein: 19 g Carbs: 65 g

19. Dark Chocolate Cheesecake

Ready in: 5 minutes

Servings: 1

Difficulty: Easy

INGREDIENTS

- 1 pouch freeze-dried dark chocolate cheesecake mix

- 1 cup water

DIRECTIONS

1. Take a pouch of chocolate cheesecake mix and make it a bowl by removing the oxygen absorber from the bottom.

2. Now boil the water in the pot and add it to the pouch.

3. Soak the mix in water for 5 minutes.

4. Stir well to settle and eat.

NUTRITION: Calories: 300 kcal Fat: 15 g Protein: 6 g Carbs: 45g

20. Cheesecake Dessert

Ready in: 10 minutes

Servings: 2

Difficulty: Easy

INGREDIENTS

- 1 can freeze-dried cheesecake

- 2 cup milk

DIRECTIONS

1. Add milk to the can of freeze-dried cheesecake.

2. Allow them to dip in milk for 10 minutes.

3. Mix them by stirring to make a thick cheesecake dessert.

4. Serve.

NUTRITION: Calories: 167 kcal Fat: 23 g Protein: 33 g Carbs: 65.5g

21. Spinach and Eggs Scramble

Ready in: 20 minutes

Servings: 2

Difficulty: Easy

INGREDIENTS

- ¼ tsp. red pepper flakes

- 2 cups fresh baby spinach leaves

- 2 tbsp. grated parmesan

- 4 large eggs

- ¼ tsp. black pepper

- ½ tsp. Diamond Crystal kosher salt

- ½ medium onion

- 2 tbsp. olive oil

DIRECTIONS

1. Take a large pan and heat the oil in it.

2. Add onion, kosher salt, and black pepper, and sauté for five minutes.

3. Add eggs, salt, parmesan, and pepper to a separate bowl and whisk together.

4. Add spinach leaves to the pan and cook for one more minute.

5. Add the egg mixture to the pan and cook for a few more minutes on medium heat.

6. Add red pepper flakes and turn off the heat.

7. Transfer the scramble to freeze dryer trays and place them in a freeze dryer.

8. Allow it to freeze dry completely.

9. Transfer the scramble to mason jars and add an oxygen absorber.

10. Close the lids and store them in a cool, dry place.

NUTRITION: Calories: 303 kcal Fat: 25 g Protein: 16 g Carbs: 4g

22. Blueberry Walnut Oat

Ready in: 5 minutes

Servings: 2 mason jars

Difficulty: Easy

INGREDIENTS

- 2 tbsp. chopped toasted walnuts

- 2 tbsp. granular no-calorie sweetener

- ½ cup blueberries

- ½ cup plain nonfat Greek-style yogurt

- ¾ cup water

- ½ cup quick-cooking oats

DIRECTIONS

1. Combine all the ingredients except for yogurt and walnuts in a bowl.

2. Place the bowl in the microwave and heat for 1 minute.

3. Add yogurt and nut and stir.

4. Transfer the oatmeal to a freeze-dryer tray and place it in a freeze-dryer.

5.   Allow it to freeze dry completely.

6.   Transfer the freeze-dried blueberry walnut oatmeal to mason jars and add an oxygen absorber.

7.   Close the lids and store them in a cool, dry place.

NUTRITION: Calories: 380 kcal Fat: 13 g Protein: 20 g Carbs: 48g

23. Organic Bac'un and Egg Scrambler

Ready in: 5 minutes

Servings: 1

Difficulty: Easy

INGREDIENTS

- 1 pack Mary Janes Farm Organic Bac'un and Egg Scrambler

- 1 cup water

DIRECTIONS

1. Take a pouch of organic Bac'un and egg scrambler and tear its notch.

2. Remove the oxygen absorber to make a bowl.

3. Add in boiling water and allow them to soak for 5 minutes.

4. Mix by stirring and serve.

NUTRITION: Calories: 140 kcal Fat: 10 g Protein: 11 g Carbs: 2g

24. Summit Breakfast Scramble

Ready in: 10 minutes

Servings: 1

Difficulty: Easy

INGREDIENTS

- 1 Freeze dried pouch summit breakfast scramble

- 1 cup water

DIRECTIONS

1. Take a pouch of freeze-dried summit breakfast scramble and tear its notch.

2. Remove the oxygen absorber to make it bowl.

3. Now add in boiling water and allow them to soak for 5 minutes.

4. Stir well to settle all the contents in it.

5. Eat and enjoy.

NUTRITION: Calories: 231 kcal Fat: 8 g Protein: 17 g Carbs: 24g

25. Granola with Milk and Blueberries

Ready in: 5 minutes

Servings: 1

Difficulty: Easy

INGREDIENTS

- 1 freeze-dried pouch granola with milk and blueberries

- ½ cup water

DIRECTIONS

1. Open the notch of the pouch and make it a bowl by removing the oxygen absorber.

2. Add in boiling water and dip for 5 minutes.

3. Stir well to mix and serve.

NUTRITION: Calories: 260 kcal Fat: 9 g Protein: 8 g Carbs: 37g

26. Yogurt Trail Mix

Ready in: 5 minutes

Servings: 1

Difficulty: Easy

INGREDIENTS

- ½ tbsp. mini semi-sweet chocolate chips

- 1 tbsp. chopped dried sweetened cranberries

- 6 oz. fat-free vanilla Greek yogurt

- ½ tbsp. dry-roasted sliced almonds

- 5 thin salted pretzel sticks

DIRECTIONS

1. Take a large bowl and add yogurt.

2. Whisk it gently using a fork to remove lumps.

3. Add the remaining ingredients to it and mix well.

4. Transfer it to freeze dryer trays and place it in a freeze dryer.

5. Allow it to freeze dry completely.

6.   Transfer it to a mason jar and add an oxygen absorber.

7.   Close the lid and store in a cool, dry place.

NUTRITION: Calories: 217 kcal Fat: 3.5 g Protein: 16.5 g Carbs: 29.5g

27. Biscuits and Gravy

Ready in: 15 minutes

Servings: 2

Difficulty: Easy

INGREDIENTS

- 15 oz. water

- 4 g freeze-dried biscuits with gravy

DIRECTIONS

1. Take a freeze-dried pouch of biscuits and gravy and open its top.

2. Remove the bottom of the pouch to make it a bowl.

3. Now boil the water in the pot and place the pouch in it.

4. Pour the boiling water into the pouch and soak them for 4 minutes.

5. Stir them well to mix and eat.

NUTRITION: Calories: 310 kcal Fat: 14 g Protein: 9 g Carbs: 35g

28. Lemon Meringue Freeze

Ready in: 1 hour 30 minutes

Servings: 10

Difficulty: Difficult

INGREDIENTS

- 4 egg whites

- 2 tbsp. sugar

- 1/4 tsp. tartar cream

- 60 ml lemon juice

- 2 tsp. corn flour

- 300ml Whipping cream

- 225g caster sugar

- 125 ml lemon juice

- 4 eggs yolk

DIRECTIONS

1. Allow the oven to preheat to 150 Fahrenheit.

2. Lined the baking trays with a baking sheet.

3. Mix the caster sugar, white eggs, corn flour, and cream of tartar to prepare the meringue discs.

4. Put the discs in the oven and bake for one hour at 140 Fahrenheit.

5. Now prepare the lemon custard on the medium by whisking whipping cream, egg yolk, lemon juice and caster sugar.

6. Now the meringue discs become cold, and place the prepared custard over it.

7. Similarly, make 2 to 3 layers and place them in the refrigerator.

8. Now prepare the lemon syrup by mixing sugar and lemon juice on simmer.

9. After removing from the refrigerator, pour the lemon syrup over the meringue discs and serve.

NUTRITION: Calories: 480 kcal Fat: 24 g Protein: 7 g Carbs: 64g

29. Chocolate Covered Strawberry Trail Mix

Ready in: 5 minutes

Servings: 5

Difficulty: Easy

INGREDIENTS

- ¾ cup almonds

- 2/3 cup dark chocolate chunks

- ¾ cup cashews

- 1 cup freeze-dried strawberries

- ¾ cup sunflower seed

DIRECTIONS

1.	Take a large bowl and mix in all the ingredients.

2.	Now put the mixture in the glass jar.

3.	Store for one month.

NUTRITION: Calories: 200 kcal Fat: 4 g Protein: 40 g Carbs: 30g

30. White Chocolate Peach and Strawberry Trail Mix

Ready in: 10 minutes

Servings: 2

Difficulty: Easy

INGREDIENTS

- 1 bag freeze dried peaches

- ¼ cup peanuts

- 1 bag of freeze-dried strawberries

- ¼ cup chocolate

- ¼ cup almonds

- ½ cup granola

DIRECTIONS

1. Take a bowl and mix in all the ingredients.

2. Store and serve whenever you want.

NUTRITION: Calories: 282 kcal Fat: 44 g Protein: 34 g Carbs: 40g

Chapter 4: Soup and Stew Recipes

1. Slow Cooker White Bean, Spinach & Sausage Stew

Ready in: 15 hours 50 minutes

Servings: 6

Difficulty: Difficult

INGREDIENTS

- 2 tbsp. extra-virgin olive oil

- ¼ cup chopped fresh flat-leaf parsley

- 5 oz. baby spinach

- 6 oz. spinach-and-feta-cheese-turkey sausage

- 2 fresh rosemary sprigs

- 4 crushed garlic cloves

- ½ tsp. black pepper

- 1 tsp. kosher salt

- 1 plum tomato

- 5 cups unsalted chicken stock

- 2 cups-dried cannellini beans

DIRECTIONS

1.   Wash the beans and place them in a Dutch oven.

2.   Add water up to two inches and let stand for eight hours.

3.   Drain the beans and transfer them to a slow cooker.

4.   Add tomato, salt, stock, pepper, rosemary sprigs, and garlic. Cover and cook on low flame for seven hours.

5.   Mash the beans using a potato masher. Add sausage and cook for two more minutes.

6.   Add spinach and parsley and stir.

7.   Remove the rosemary sprigs and drizzle with oil.

8.   Transfer the stew to freeze dryer trays and place in a freeze dryer.

9.   Allow the stew to freeze dry completely.

10.   Transfer to mason jars and add oxygen absorber.

11.   Close the lids and store them in a cool, dry place.

NUTRITION: Calories: 314 kcal Fat: 9 g Protein: 21 g Carbs: 39g

2. Tomato and Basil Soup

Ready in: 30 minutes

Servings: 4

Difficulty: Easy

INGREDIENTS

- ½ cup basil leaves

- 142 ml pot soured cream

- 500 ml turkey or vegetable stock

- 5 chopped soft sundried or SunBlush tomatoes in oil

- 1 tbsp. butter

- 125 g pot fresh basil pesto

- 1 tsp. sugar

- Three 400 g cans of plum tomatoes

- 2 crushed garlic cloves

DIRECTIONS

1. Take a pan and heat butter in it. Add garlic and sauté for a few minutes.

2.   Add canned tomatoes, sundried or Sun Blush tomatoes, sugar, stock and seasoning to the pan and bring to a boil.

3.   Allow the mixture to simmer for ten minutes.

4.   Blend the mixture using a hand blender while adding soured cream to it.

5.   Pour the soup into an ice cube tray and add some pesto and basil leaves on top of each.

6.   Place the tray in the freezer for some time.

7.   Transfer the cubes to freeze dryer trays lined with parchment paper and place them in a freeze dryer.

8.   Allow them to freeze dry completely.

9.   Remove the tray and transfer the soup cubes to jars and add an oxygen absorber to each.

10.   Close the lids and store them in a cool, dry place.

NUTRITION: Calories: 213 kcal Fat: 14 g Protein: 8 g Carbs: 14g

3. Spinach and Parmesan Frittatas Vegan Soup

Ready in: 20 minutes

Servings: 4

Difficulty: Easy

INGREDIENTS

- 1/8 tsp. black pepper

- ¾ tsp. salt

- 6 eggs

- ½ cup feta cheese

- 1 lb. frozen spinach

DIRECTIONS

1.   Allow the oven to preheat to 375 Fahrenheit.

2.   Take a baking dish and line it with parchment paper.

3.   Add spinach to a colander and drain water.

4.   Add eggs, salt and black pepper to a bowl and whisk together.

5.   Add spinach and crumbled feta to the baking dish and pour the egg mixture over them.

6.   Bake for fifteen minutes.

7.   Transfer the frittatas to freeze dryer trays and place them in a freeze dryer.

8.   Allow them to freeze dry completely.

9.   Transfer them to airtight containers and add an oxygen absorber.

10.   Close the lid and store in a cool, dry place.

NUTRITION: Calories: 177 kcal Fat: 11 g Protein: 15 g Carbs: 6g

4. Thai Coconut Milk Soup

Ready in: 1 hour 15 minutes

Servings: 8

Difficulty: Difficult

INGREDIENTS

- ¼ cup chopped fresh cilantro

- 2 tbsp. fresh lime juice

- ¾ tsp. salt

- 1 lb. peeled medium shrimp

- ½ lb. sliced shiitake mushroom

- Three 13.5 oz. cans of coconut milk

- 1 tbsp. light brown sugar

- 3 tbsp. fish sauce

- 4 cups chicken broth

- 2 tsp. red curry paste

- 1 stalk lemon grass, minced

- 2 tbsp. grated fresh ginger

- 1 tbsp. vegetable oil

DIRECTIONS

1. Take a large pan and heat the oil in it. Add ginger, lemongrass and curry paste and cook for one minute.

2. Add chicken broth, fish sauce, and brown sugar, and let the mixture simmer for fifteen minutes.

3. Add coconut milk and mushrooms and cook for five more minutes.

4. Add shrimp, lime juice and salt and cook the mixture for a few more minutes.

5. Add cilantro for garnishing.

6. Transfer the soup to freeze-drying trays and place it in a freeze-dryer.

7. Remove the trays and transfer the crumbles to mason jars.

8. Add an oxygen absorber and close the lids.

9. Store in a cool, dry place.

NUTRITION: Calories: 368 kcal Fat: 32.9 g Protein: 13.2 g Carbs: 8.9g

5. Tomato Soup with Whole Wheat Orzo

Ready in: 30 minutes

Servings: 6

Difficulty: Easy

INGREDIENTS

- ¾ cup uncooked whole wheat orzo

- 1 tsp. brown sugar

- 14.5 oz. diced tomatoes

- ½ tsp. dried basil

- 1 medium grated carrot

- 1 tbsp. extra virgin olive oil

- ¾ cup plain non fat Greek yogurt

- 1 cup water

- ½ tsp. red pepper flakes

- 1 bay leaf

- ½ tsp. salt

- ½ tsp. black pepper

- 1 small minced yellow onion

- ½ cup Cheddar cheese

- ½ cup fresh herbs for garnishing

DIRECTIONS

1. Heat oil in a pan and add onions, carrot, salt, pepper, and sauté.

2. Add bay leaf, red pepper flakes, basil, water, brown sugar and tomatoes to the pan and bring to a boil.

3. Let the mixture simmer for fifteen minutes on low heat.

4. In the meantime, cook orzo as directed on the package.

5. Remove the pan from heat, add orzo and Greek yogurt, and stir.

6. Add cheddar cheese and fresh herbs on top.

7. Transfer the soup to freeze dryer trays and allow it to freeze dry completely.

8. Transfer to mason jars.

9. Add an oxygen absorber to each jar and close the lids. NUTRITION: Calories: 210 kcal Fat: 5 g Protein: 10 g Carbs: 33g

6. Slow Cooker Brazilian Pork and Black Bean Stew

Ready in: 5 hours and 30 minutes

Servings: 8

Difficulty: Difficult

INGREDIENTS

- ½ tsp. salt

- ½ tsp. pepper

- 2 bay leaves

- 1 lb. dried black beans

- 1 cup water

- 2 tsp ground cumin

- 6 minced garlic cloves

- 3 minced onions

- 3 lb. boneless pork butt, trimmed and cut into chunks

- 1 lb. sliced kielbasa

- 4 cups low sodium chicken broth

- 1 tsp. ground coriander

- 2 tbsp. chili powder

- ¼ cup tomato paste

- 6 oz. minced bacon

DIRECTIONS

1. Take a large pan and add bacon to it. Cook for five minutes.

2. Add onion, garlic, tomato paste, cumin, coriander and chili powder, and cook for ten more minutes.

3. Add water and stir.

4. Transfer the mixture to a slow cooker.

5. Add beans, bay leaves, kielbasa and broth and stir.

6. Take the pork, sprinkle it with salt and pepper, and then transfer it to the slow cooker.

7. Cover the cooker and cook the mixture for 5 hours on high flame.

8. Turn off the heat and let the stew settle.

9. Remove fat from the surface and bay leaves.

10. Add Brazilian hot sauce and mix.

11. Transfer the stew to freeze dryer trays and place in a freeze dryer.

12. Allow the stew to freeze dry completely.

13. Remove the trays and transfer the stew to mason jars.

14. Add an oxygen absorber to each jar and close the lids.

15. Store in a cool, dry place away from direct sunlight.

NUTRITION: Calories: 898.4 kcal Fat: 53.8 g Protein: 57.3 g
Carbs: 46.2g

7. Gluten-Free, Grain-Free Lemon Chicken Soup

Ready in: 40 minutes

Servings: 4

Difficulty: Medium

INGREDIENTS

- 1 cup chopped kale

- ½ cup lemon juice

- 3 egg yolks

- ½ tsp. black pepper

- 1 tsp. salt

- 2 tbsp. fresh parsley

- 1 tsp. dried dill

- 12 oz. shredded and precooked chicken

- 6 cups chicken broth

- 2 cups riced cauliflower

- 1 cup diced carrot

- 3 minced garlic cloves

- 1 diced yellow onion

- 2 tbsp. olive oil

DIRECTIONS

1. Take a large pot and heat the oil in it.

2. Add onions and sauté for three minutes.

3. Add carrots and cauliflower rice and fry for five more minutes.

4. Add chicken broth and herbs and bring to a boil.

5. Let the mixture simmer for ten minutes.

6. Take out a cup of hot broth and set it aside.

7. Whisk the egg yolks in a separate bowl and pour the hot broth in it while whisking.

8. Add the egg and broth mixture to the pot and stir.

9. Add lemon juice and chicken and let the soup simmer for ten more minutes.

10. Add kale and allow it to cook for two minutes.

11. Turn off the heat and allow it to cool.

12. Transfer the soup to freeze dryer trays and place in a freeze dryer.

13.	Allow it to freeze dry completely.

14.	Transfer the freeze-dried soup to mason jars and add an oxygen absorber.

15.	Close the lids and store them in a cool, dry place.

NUTRITION: Calories: 279 kcal Fat: 13.1 g Protein: 28.5 g Carbs: 13.3g

8. Hearty Chicken and Veggie Soup

Ready in: 1 hour 15 minutes

Servings: 6

Difficulty: Difficult

INGREDIENTS

- ¾ cup parmesan cheese

- 1 pinch salt

- 1 pinch pepper

- 2 tbsp. parsley

- 1 tbsp. lemon juice

- ½ cup fregola pasta

- 150 g sweet corn

- 1 zucchini

- 4 tbsp. tomato paste

- 2 lbs. chicken tenders

- 6 cups hot chicken stock

- 1 tsp. dried thyme

- 1 tsp. salt

- 1 cup cubed butternut squash

- 1 large potato

- 3 carrots

- 4 celery sticks

- 1 large onion

- 1 tbsp. olive oil

DIRECTIONS

1. Take a large pan and heat the oil in it.

2. Add onions, carrots, potato, celery, and squash to it and fry for five minutes.

3. Add stock and bring the mixture to a boil.

4. Add chicken and tomato paste and let the mixture simmer for fifteen minutes.

5. Add zucchini, lemon juice, pasta and corn and cook for ten more minutes.

6. Turn off the heat and shred the chicken using a fork.

7. Add parsley and parmesan cheese and stir.

8. Transfer the soup to freeze dryer trays and place in a freeze dryer.

9.   Allow it to freeze dry completely.

10.   Transfer the soup to mason jars and add an oxygen absorber.

11.   Close the lids and store them in a cool, dry place.

NUTRITION: Calories: 203 kcal Fat: 3 g Protein: 6 g Carbs: 38g

9. Baked potato, cheese, and onion soup

Ready in: 1 hour

Servings: 8

Difficulty: Difficult

INGREDIENTS

- 6 cups potatoes

- ½ cup cheddar cheese

- 1 onion

- 2 tbsp. ranch dressing

- 1 tbsp. chicken bouillon

- ½ tsp. Onion powder

- ½ cup butter

- ½ tsp. Pepper

- ½ cup flour

- Salt as required

- 6 cups milk

- 1/3 cup sour cream

- 2 cans corn

DIRECTIONS

1. Take a pot and add onion and potatoes, and bouillon by stirring.

2. Allow them to boil until potatoes are tender.

3. Over medium heat, allow the butter to melt in a stock pot.

4. Put in the flour and mix until smooth.

5. Now pour in milk by whisking gradually.

6. Now add in boiled onion and potato mixture along with corn.

7. Allow them to boil, and then set them to simmer.

8. Now add in bacon and sour cream by stirring

9. Serve or freeze for future use.

NUTRITION: Calories: 418 kcal Fat: 20 g Protein: 12 g Carbs: 47g

10. Freeze Dried Potatoes with Chive Soup

Ready in: 25 minutes

Servings: 2

Difficulty: Easy

INGREDIENTS

- 1/3 cup instant potato flakes

- 1-3/4 cup boiling water

- 2 tbsp. parmesan cheese

- 1/8 tsp. salt

- 1 tsp. corn starch

- 1/8 tsp. black pepper

- 1 tbsp. freeze-dried chives

- 1/8 tsp. onion powder

- 2 tbsp. chicken powder

- 1/8 tsp. garlic powder

- ¼ cup buttermilk powder

DIRECTIONS

1. Take a freezer Ziplock bag and mix in all the ingredients except water.

2. Allow the water to boil and place the opened Ziplock bag in the water.

3. Now pour boiling water into the bag.

4. Soak the mixture in the boiling water for 10 minutes.

5. Whisk and wat soup from the bag.

NUTRITION: Calories: 200 kcal Fat: 34 g Protein: 32 g Carbs: 11g

11. Organic Green Lentil Soup

Ready in: 10 minutes

Servings: 1

Difficulty: Easy

INGREDIENTS

- 1 pouch freeze-dried organic green lentil soup

- 2 cups boiling water

DIRECTIONS

1. Take a pouch of freeze-dried organic green lentil soup and pour it into boiling water.

2. Allow them to soak for 5 minutes.

3. Now stir them well to blend it.

4. Eat and enjoy.

NUTRITION: Calories: 210 kcal Fat: 1.5 g Protein: 13 g Carbs: 40g

12. Stuffed Pepper Soup

Ready in: 45 minutes

Servings: 8

Difficulty: Easy

INGREDIENTS

- 2 lb. beef, grounded

- ½ tsp. Kosher salt

- 2 tbsp. olive oil

- 2 tsp. dried oregano

- 1 onion

- 2 tsp. ground cumin

- 6 garlic cloves

- 32 oz. beef broth

- 2 red bell peppers

- 2 cans of tomato juice

- 2 green bell pepper

1. Preheat the oven and brown the beef until completely cooked.

2. Now cook the onion in olive oil over medium heat.

3. Cook in garlic for one minute, and add black pepper, salt, and peppers.

4. Put in oregano, tomatoes, cumin, broth, and juice to simmer for 30 minutes with a closed top.

5. Once done, ladle soup into the bowl with cooked beef.

6. Serve.

NUTRITION: Calories: 231 kcal Fat: 7.4 g Protein: 26.9 g Carbs: 14.6g

COOKING CONVERSION CHART

WEIGHT

IMPERIAL	METRIC
1/2 oz	15 g
1 oz	29 g
2 oz	57 g
3 oz	85 g
4 oz	113 g
5 oz	141 g
6 oz	170 g
8 oz	227 g
10 oz	283 g
12 oz	340 g
13 oz	369 g
14 oz	397 g
15 oz	425 g
1 lb	453 g

TEMPERATURE

FAHRENHEIT	CELSIUS
100 °F	37 °C
150 °F	65 °C
200 °F	93 °C
250 °F	121 °C
300 °F	150 °C
325 °F	160 °C
350 °F	180 °C
375 °F	190 °C
400 °F	200 °C
425 °F	220 °C
450 °F	230 °C
500 °F	260 °C
525 °F	274 °C
550 °F	288 °C

MEASUREMENT

CUP	ONCES	MILLILITERS	TBSP
8 cup	64 oz	1895 ml	128
6 cup	48 oz	1420 ml	96
5 cup	40 oz	1180 ml	80
4 cup	32 oz	960 ml	64
2 cup	16 oz	500 ml	32
1 cup	8 oz	250 ml	16
3/4 cup	6 oz	177 ml	12
2/3 cup	5 oz	158 ml	11
1/2 cup	4 oz	118 ml	8
3/8 cup	3 oz	90 ml	6
1/3 cup	2.5 oz	79 ml	5.5
1/4 cup	2 oz	59 ml	4
1/8 cup	1 oz	30 ml	3
1/16 cup	1/2 oz	15 ml	1

Conclusion

To conclude, freeze-drying is a technique that helps preserve food by removing moisture. It is a kind of dehydration process which occurs in two steps.

i.   Freezing food below its glass transition temperature.

ii.   Making food goes through a vacuum cycle which removes all the moisture from the food. Moisture in the form of ice is directly converted to a vapor state without converting to liquid.

Freeze drying has various advantages over other preservation techniques, such as:

i.   The food is lightweight and easy to carry around.

ii.   High temperature is not required during freeze drying; therefore, heat sensitive components of food remain intact.

iii.   The freeze-dried food item can be stored for up to twenty-five years.

iv.   Freeze drying process preserves the taste and nutrients in the food as well.

Freeze drying can be done using either a freeze-dryer machine such as Harvest Right freeze dryer or without a freeze-drying machine by adopting a DIY freeze-drying method at home.

Freeze drying machines are more convenient for the large-scale freeze-drying process. They usually have different freeze dryer trays for different food items, making the process much quicker and easier.

One thing that should be kept in mind while adopting freeze drying is that it is a time taking process. It may take several hours to days, depending on the type of food. Therefore, if there is a shortage of time, it is better to adopt some other method of food preservation, such as pressure or water bath, which are less time-consuming.